THE AUSTRALIAN
Women's Weekly

SUPERFOODS

THE AUSTRALIAN WOMEN'S WEEKLY
TRIPLE TESTED
TEST KITCHEN

contents

12 large-scale studies found a strong association between intake of whole grains and up to 30 per cent reduced risk of type 2 diabetes.

Diversify your intake of whole grains. Choose from **barley, brown rice, freekeh, oats, rye** or the ancient grains **spelt** and **kamut.**

Quinoa is cooked and eaten as a grain alternative but is in fact the seed of a leafy plant similar to spinach. It has a delicate, slightly nutty taste and chewy texture. It is available from most supermarkets and health-food stores.

SUPER GRAINS

Grains are a staple food of a majority of diverse cultures around the world and have been for about 10,000 years. Big population studies have consistently shown that eating whole grains is good for us, reducing our risk of chronic diseases including heart disease, diabetes, stroke and certain cancers, and helping us to live longer.

Whole grains

do not deserve to be thrown into the same nutrition basket as products based on white flour. The breads and cereals group was the second most important source of protein in the Australian diet in our last nutrition survey. It was also the largest source of fibre, thiamin, magnesium and iron. Where we can certainly go wrong is the form in which we eat our grains.

Whole grains contain all three parts of the grain kernel — the bran, germ and endosperm — whereas the process used to make white flour removes the outer layers and only the starchy centre, the endosperm, is used. Unfortunately this process removes a large percentage of the grain nutrients and phytochemicals, along with the fibre. The end result is a refined starch product that inevitably has a high GI.

rice

crunchy asian rice salad

PREP + COOK TIME 15 MINUTES • SERVES 4

500g (1 pound) packaged quick-cook brown basmati rice

1 lebanese cucumber (130g)

½ small wombok (napa cabbage) (350g), shredded

100g (3 ounces) snow peas, sliced thinly

1 small carrot (70g), cut into long thin strips

2 cups (160g) bean sprouts

2 green onions (scallions), sliced thinly

½ cup (70g) salted peanuts, chopped coarsely

¼ cup loosely packed fresh perilla leaves, torn

¼ cup loosely packed fresh thai basil leaves, torn

SESAME DRESSING

2 tablespoons kecap manis

¼ cup (70g) tahini

1 teaspoon sesame oil

2 tablespoons mirin

2 tablespoons water

1 Heat rice in a microwave oven according to packet instructions.

2 Meanwhile, halve cucumber lengthways; remove seeds. Cut cucumber into long thin strips.

3 Place rice and cucumber in a large bowl with wombok, snow peas, carrot and sprouts, then most of the onion, peanuts, perilla and thai basil; toss gently to combine.

4 Make sesame dressing.

5 Add dressing to salad; toss gently to combine. Top salad with remaining onion, peanuts, perilla and thai basil.

SESAME DRESSING Whisk ingredients together in a small bowl.

Test Kitchen
NOTES

Vine leaves are available
from Middle Eastern
food shops and some
delicatessens. If vine
leaves are too small use
two leaves together.

brown rice and pine nut stuffed vine leaves

1 cup (200g) medium-grain brown rice

1½ cups (375ml) water

½ cup (80g) pine nuts

20g (¾ ounce) butter

1 medium brown onion (150g), chopped finely

1 teaspoon ground coriander

½ cup (80g) dried currants

120g (4 ounces) labne

½ cup loosely packed fresh mint leaves, chopped finely

½ cup loosely packed fresh dill leaves, chopped finely

2 teaspoons finely grated lemon rind

2 tablespoons lemon juice

¾ cup (200g) Greek-style yoghurt

28 preserved vine leaves, approximately

1 teaspoon sumac

1 Bring rice and the water to the boil in a medium saucepan; cook, covered, over low heat for 25 minutes or until tender. Remove from heat; stand, covered, 10 minutes.

2 Meanwhile, stir pine nuts in a medium frying pan over medium heat until lightly toasted. Transfer to a large bowl.

3 Heat butter in same frying pan over medium heat; cook onion and coriander, stirring, until browned and soft.

4 Add onion mixture and rice to pine nuts with currants, labne, herbs, rind and half the juice; stir to combine. Season to taste.

5 Combine yoghurt and remaining juice in a small serving bowl; season to taste.

6 Rinse vine leaves in cold water. Drop leaves into a large saucepan of boiling water, in batches, for a few seconds, transfer to a colander; rinse under cold water, drain well. Place a vine leaf, smooth-side down, on bench; trim large stem. Place a tablespoon of rice mixture in centre. Fold stem end and sides over filling; roll up firmly. Repeat with remaining vine leaves and rice mixture.

7 Serve rolls drizzled with olive oil and scattered with extra mint leaves, if you like. Accompany with yoghurt mixture sprinkled with sumac.

vietnamese pancakes with prawns

8 cooked tiger prawns (shrimp) (280g)

½ cup (90g) rice flour

¼ teaspoon turmeric

2 tablespoons coconut milk

⅔ cup (160ml) water

1 egg

1 tablespoon olive oil

8 butter (boston) lettuce leaves (pulled from the centre of the lettuce)

1 lebanese cucumber (130g), sliced thinly

1 medium carrot (120g), sliced into ribbons

1 cup (80g) bean sprouts

½ bunch fresh mint leaves

½ bunch fresh thai basil leaves

CHILLI DIPPING SAUCE

1 tablespoon warm water

1 tablespoon lemon juice

2 teaspoons cane sugar

½ teaspoon fish sauce

½ clove garlic, crushed

1 fresh small red thai chilli (serrano), chopped finely

1 Make chilli dipping sauce.

2 Shell and devein prawns leaving tails intact.

3 Place rice flour and turmeric in a medium bowl. Add coconut milk, the water and egg; whisk until well combined and batter is smooth.

4 Heat 1 teaspoon of the oil in a large non-stick frying pan (base measurement 23cm/9 inches) over medium heat; pour a quarter of the batter into pan, swirl around base to form a thin pancake. Cook for 2 minutes or until batter has set.

5 Slide pancake onto a serving plate and repeat to make three more pancakes.

6 Serve pancakes with prawns, lettuce, cucumber, carrot, sprouts, herbs and chilli dipping sauce.

CHILLI DIPPING SAUCE Place the warm water, juice and sugar in a small bowl; stir until sugar has dissolved. Add remaining ingredients; stir to combine.

brown fried rice with carrot, cabbage and red onion

1⅓ cups (265g) medium-grain brown rice

1 tablespoon peanut oil

2 eggs, beaten lightly

3 small carrots (200g)

1 medium red onion (170g), cut into wedges

300g (9½ ounces) red cabbage, shredded coarsely

2 cloves garlic, crushed

1 tablespoon finely grated fresh ginger (20g)

2 green onions (scallions), sliced thinly

1½ tablespoons light soy sauce

1 fresh long red chilli, sliced thinly

1 Cook rice in a medium saucepan of boiling salted water for 35 minutes or until tender; drain. Rinse under cold water; drain well.

2 Meanwhile, heat a large wok on medium-high heat; add 1 teaspoon of the oil, swirl to coat wok. Add egg; swirl wok to make a thin omelette. Cook for 30 seconds or until just set; slide omelette onto a clean board. Roll tightly; cut into strips.

3 Thinly slice carrots on the diagonal.

4 Heat remaining oil in same wok; stir-fry carrot and red onion for 4 minutes or until just tender. Add cabbage; stir-fry for 2 minutes or until wilted. Add garlic, ginger and half the green onion; stir-fry until fragrant. Add rice and sauce; stir-fry until hot.

5 Serve fried rice topped with omelette strips, chilli and remaining green onion.

mediterranean grain salad with honey cumin labne

PREP + COOK TIME 1 HOUR • SERVES 6

¾ cup (150g) brown rice

½ cup (100g) french-style green lentils

½ cup (100g) red or white quinoa

1 cup (250ml) water

1 small red onion (100g), chopped finely

2 tablespoons pepitas (pumpkin seeds), toasted

2 tablespoons sunflower seeds, toasted

2 tablespoons pine nuts, toasted

2 tablespoons salted baby capers, rinsed

½ cup (80g) currants

1 cup firmly packed fresh flat-leaf parsley leaves

1 cup firmly packed fresh coriander (cilantro) leaves

¼ cup (60ml) lemon juice

⅓ cup (80ml) olive oil

1 teaspoon cumin seeds, toasted

1 cup (280g) labne

1½ tablespoons honey

½ cup (40g) flaked almonds, roasted

1 Cook rice and lentils, separately, in large saucepans of boiling water for 25 minutes or until tender; drain, rinse well.

2 Place quinoa in a small saucepan with the water; bring to the boil. Reduce heat to low; simmer, covered, for 10 minutes or until tender. Drain.

3 Combine rice, lentils and quinoa in a large bowl. Add onion, pepitas, sunflower seeds, pine nuts, capers, currants, herbs, juice and oil; stir until well combined.

4 Stir cumin seeds into labne in a small bowl.

5 Serve salad topped with spoonfuls of labne, drizzle with honey and scatter with nuts.

Test Kitchen NOTES

Toast and roast seeds and nuts together on an oven tray (place the cumin seeds on a small piece of foil to keep them separate), in a 180°C/350°F oven about 8 minutes, stirring halfway through cooking time.

Sashimi-grade fish must be impeccably fresh and prepared using extremely strict standards of hygiene as it is to be eaten raw. If you are unable to obtain it, or prefer your fish cooked, simply cook the fish a further 1½ minutes on each side or until cooked through.

seared wasabi salmon and brown rice salad

PREP + COOK TIME 20 MINUTES • SERVES 4

500g (1 pound) packaged pre-cooked brown basmati rice

350g (11 ounces) sashimi-grade salmon

2 tablespoons sesame seeds

1 tablespoon wasabi powder

2 tablespoons olive oil

100g (3 ounces) baby asian salad leaves

¼ cup (70g) pickled ginger

2 green onions (scallions), sliced thinly

1 fresh long red chilli, sliced thinly

1 large avocado (320g), chopped

2 tablespoons light soy sauce

2 tablespoons lime juice

1 tablespoon olive oil, extra

1 lime, cut into wedges

1 Reheat rice following packet instructions; cool slightly.

2 Meanwhile, roll salmon in combined sesame seeds and wasabi powder until coated.

3 Heat oil in a large frying pan over high heat; cook salmon for 1 minute each side or until browned but still raw in the centre. Cool 5 minutes. Slice thinly.

4 Place rice in a large bowl with salad leaves, ginger, onion, chilli and avocado; toss gently to combine.

5 Place sauce, juice and extra oil in a screw-top jar; shake well.

6 Arrange rice salad and salmon on a platter; drizzle with dressing. Serve with lime.

Test Kitchen
NOTES

You will need to cook
1½ cups (300g) brown
rice for this recipe.

soft-boiled egg and brown rice nasi goreng

PREP + COOK TIME 45 MINUTES • SERVES 4

400g (12½ ounces) gai lan

375g (12 ounces) choy sum

½ cup firmly packed fresh coriander (cilantro) leaves

4 eggs

2 tablespoons peanut oil

6 shallots (150g), halved, sliced thinly

4cm (1½-inch) piece fresh ginger (20g), cut into thin matchsticks

2 cloves garlic, crushed

2 fresh long red chillies, sliced thinly

150g (4½ ounces) button mushrooms, quartered

100g (3 ounces) shiitake mushrooms, sliced thinly

115g (3½ ounces) baby corn, halved lengthways

3½ cups (625g) cooked brown rice

1 teaspoon sesame oil

2 tablespoons kecap manis

1 Cut stalks from gai lan and choy sum. Cut stalks into 10cm (4-inch) lengths; cut leaves into 10cm (4-inch) pieces. Keep stalks and leaves separated. Chop half the coriander; reserve remaining leaves.
2 Cook eggs in a medium saucepan of boiling water for 5 minutes or until soft-boiled; drain. When cool enough to handle, peel eggs.
3 Meanwhile, heat half the peanut oil in a wok over medium heat; stir-fry shallots for 8 minutes or until soft and light golden. Add ginger, garlic and half the chilli; stir-fry for 4 minutes or until softened. Transfer mixture to a plate.
4 Heat remaining peanut oil in wok over medium-high heat; stir-fry mushrooms and corn for 4 minutes or until just tender. Add asian green stalks; stir-fry about 3 minutes. Add asian green leaves, rice, sesame oil, kecap manis, shallot mixture and chopped coriander; stir-fry for 3 minutes or until rice is hot and leaves are wilted. Season to taste.
5 Serve nasi goreng topped with reserved coriander leaves, remaining chilli and eggs.

spiced lamb pilaf

1½ cups (300g) basmati rice

1 litre (4 cups) water

1 tablespoon olive oil

3 lamb leg steaks (450g), sliced thinly

1 medium brown onion (150g), sliced thinly

2 cloves garlic, sliced thinly

1 tablespoon finely grated fresh ginger

2 dried bay leaves

2 teaspoons ground coriander

½ teaspoon ground cinnamon

½ cup (75g) coarsely chopped dried apricots

2¼ cups (560ml) chicken stock

¼ cup (35g) roasted unsalted shelled pistachios, chopped coarsely

½ cup loosely packed fresh mint leaves

1 cup (280g) Greek-style yoghurt

1 Cover rice in a medium bowl with the water; stand 30 minutes. Drain well.

2 Meanwhile, heat oil in a large saucepan; cook lamb, in batches, until browned. Remove from pan.

3 Cook onion in same pan, stirring, until softened. Add garlic, ginger, bay leaves and spices; cook, stirring, until fragrant. Stir in rice. Add apricot and stock; bring to the boil. Reduce heat; cook, covered, over low heat, for 20 minutes or until rice is tender.

4 Stir lamb into pilaf; season to taste. Sprinkle with nuts and mint; serve with yoghurt.

basic risotto

1 litre (4 cups) chicken stock

½ cup (125ml) dry white or red wine

¼ cup (60ml) olive oil

100g (3 ounces) butter, chopped

1 small brown onion (80g), chopped finely

2 cloves garlic, crushed

1½ cups (300g) carnaroli or arborio rice

½ cup (40g) finely grated parmesan

1 Place stock and wine in a medium saucepan; bring to a simmer over medium heat and keep at a gentle simmer.

2 Heat oil and half the butter in a heavy-based medium saucepan over medium heat; cook onion and garlic, stirring, for 5 minutes or until onion is soft. Add rice; stir for 2 minutes or until rice is well coated in oil. Stir in 1 cup hot stock mixture until liquid is absorbed. Continue adding stock mixture, 1 cup at a time, stirring frequently, until liquid is absorbed after each addition. Stir in remaining butter and parmesan until melted. Serve immediately.

Test Kitchen
NOTES

Thai sticky rice (also known as 'glutinous' or 'sweet' rice) is a short, fat and chalky white rice that becomes soft and sticky once cooked. If you don't have time to soak the rice overnight, serve the salad with steamed jasmine rice or soaked vermicelli noodles instead. You can use green papaya instead of the mango and apple, if you like.

sticky rice with green mango and apple salad

PREP + COOK TIME 40 MINUTES (+ STANDING) • SERVES 4

You will need to start this recipe the day before.

2 cups (400g) sticky (glutinous) rice

½ cup (25g) moist coconut flakes

2 green mangoes (660g), peeled

2 medium green-skinned apples (300g)

1 shallot (25g), sliced finely

2 fresh long red chillies, seeded, sliced thinly

4 fresh kaffir lime leaves, sliced thinly

½ cup (70g) salted peanuts, chopped coarsely

⅓ cup firmly packed fresh coriander (cilantro) leaves

⅓ cup (80ml) lime juice

½ teaspoon sesame oil

1 tablespoon rice wine vinegar

2 teaspoons finely grated palm sugar

½ teaspoon salt

1 fresh kaffir lime leaf, extra, sliced finely

1 Rinse rice in a sieve or colander under cold water until water runs clear. Place rice in a large bowl of cold water overnight.

2 Drain rice. Place rice in a muslin-lined metal or bamboo steamer; cover tightly. Place steamer over a large wok or saucepan of boiling water, making sure the bottom of the steamer does not touch the water. Steam rice, tightly covered, for 35 minutes or until tender. Do not remove lid from the steamer or stir rice during cooking; check the water level occasionally, topping up with boiling water if needed.

3 Meanwhile, stir coconut in a large frying pan over high heat until toasted lightly. Remove from pan.

4 Cut mangoes and apples into matchsticks; place in a large bowl with shallot, chilli, lime leaves, peanuts, coriander and ⅓ cup of the toasted coconut. Add combined juice, oil, vinegar, sugar and salt; toss gently to combine.

5 Serve sticky rice with salad; sprinkle with remaining coconut and extra lime leaf.

4 ways with RISOTTO

fennel, lemon and scallop risotto

PREP + COOK TIME 45 MINUTES • **SERVES** 4

Make one quantity basic risotto (recipe page 19), omitting the parmesan. Heat 30g (1 ounce) butter in a frying pan over medium heat; cook 1 finely chopped bulb baby fennel for 5 minutes or until tender. Season. Stir fennel mixture into risotto with finely grated rind of 1 lemon and 2 tablespoons finely chopped fresh chives. Heat 30g (1 ounce) butter in same pan over medium heat; cook 400g (12½ ounces) scallops, in batches, for 1 minute each side or until just tender. Serve risotto immediately, topped with scallops and fennel fronds.

red wine, pumpkin and rosemary risotto

PREP + COOK TIME 50 MINUTES • **SERVES** 4

Make one quantity basic risotto (recipe page 19) with red wine. Preheat oven to 190°C/375°F. Cut 500g (1 pound) peeled and seeded butternut pumpkin into 1cm (½-inch) pieces; toss with 1 tablespoon olive oil and 1½ teaspoons fresh rosemary in a roasting pan. Season. Roast for 35 minutes or until tender. Stir half the pumpkin mixture into risotto. Serve risotto immediately, topped with remaining pumpkin.

cabbage, pancetta and gorgonzola risotto

PREP + COOK TIME 50 MINUTES • **SERVES** 4

Make one quantity basic risotto (recipe page 19). Heat 1 tablespoon olive oil in a frying pan over medium heat; cook 150g (4½ ounces) pancetta cut into 6mm (¼-inch) pieces, stirring, about 5 minutes. Stir in 400g (12½ ounces) shredded savoy cabbage (about ¼ cabbage); cook, covered, about 10 minutes. Season. Stir cabbage mixture into risotto with 40g (1½ ounces) crumbled gorgonzola cheese. Serve immediately, topped with fresh flat-leaf parsley leaves.

smoked salmon, spinach and mascarpone risotto

PREP + COOK TIME 45 MINUTES • **SERVES** 4

Make one quantity basic risotto (recipe page 19), omitting the parmesan. Heat 1 tablespoon olive oil in a frying pan over medium heat; cook 2 thinly sliced green onions (scallions) and 1 cup baby spinach leaves, stirring, for 2 minutes or until spinach is just wilted. Stir spinach mixture into risotto with 100g (3 ounces) thinly sliced smoked salmon. Top risotto with 100g (3 ounces) smoked salmon torn into pieces and 1 tablespoon mascarpone cheese. Serve sprinkled with 2 tablespoons chopped fresh dill.

quinoa and barley

quinoa salad with haloumi and pomegranate

PREP + COOK TIME 25 MINUTES • SERVES 4

1 cup (200g) red or white quinoa

2 cups (500ml) water

1 clove garlic, crushed

2 tablespoons lemon juice

2 teaspoons each ground cumin and ground coriander

¼ cup (60ml) olive oil

½ cup loosely packed fresh mint leaves

100g (3 ounces) baby spinach leaves

½ cup (75g) sunflower seeds, toasted

250g (8 ounces) haloumi, cut into 1cm (½-inch) slices

¾ cup (210g) Greek-style yoghurt

⅓ cup (50g) pomegranate seeds

1 Bring quinoa and the water to the boil in a medium saucepan; cook, covered, over low heat for 15 minutes or until tender. Drain; cool slightly.

2 Combine garlic, juice, spices and 1 tablespoon of the oil in a large bowl; season to taste. Add quinoa to bowl with mint, spinach leaves and sunflower seeds; toss gently to combine.

3 Heat remaining oil in a large frying pan over high heat; cook haloumi for 1 minute each side or until golden.

4 Serve quinoa salad topped with haloumi, yoghurt and pomegranate seeds.

For something different, swap the quinoa for lentils, freekeh or barley.

Test Kitchen
NOTES

Cook the haloumi just before serving as it becomes tough and rubbery on cooling. Fresh pomegranate seeds can sometimes be found in the fridge section of supermarkets. If unavailable, cut a whole pomegranate in half and scrape the seeds from the flesh with your fingers while holding the pomegranate upside down in a bowl of cold water; the seeds will sink and the white pith will float.

Test Kitchen
NOTES

Cavolo nero is also known
as tuscan cabbage; it is
highly nutritious and is
also great to use in soups,
salads and stir-fries.

mushroom, cavolo nero and quinoa risotto

PREP + COOK TIME 40 MINUTES · SERVES 4

20g (¾ ounce) dried porcini mushrooms

1 cup (250ml) boiling water

1 tablespoon olive oil

1 medium brown onion (150g), chopped finely

2 flat mushrooms (160g), chopped coarsely

200g (6½ ounces) swiss brown mushrooms, sliced thinly

2 cloves garlic, crushed

1 cup quinoa (200g), rinsed, drained

1.25 litres (5 cups) vegetable stock

2 sprigs fresh thyme

200g (6½ ounces) cavolo nero, sliced thinly

⅓ cup (25g) grated parmesan

⅓ cup (25g) flaked parmesan

1 Place porcini mushrooms in a heatproof bowl; cover with the boiling water. Stand 5 minutes.

2 Meanwhile, heat oil in a medium frying pan over medium heat; cook onion, stirring, for 3 minutes or until soft. Add flat and swiss brown mushrooms; cook, stirring, for 3 minutes or until browned and tender. Add garlic; cook, stirring, for 1 minute or until fragrant. Stir in quinoa, stock and thyme.

3 Remove porcini mushrooms from water (reserve the soaking liquid); chop coarsely. Add mushrooms and soaking liquid to pan. Bring to the boil; simmer, uncovered for 20 minutes or until liquid is absorbed and quinoa is tender. Discard thyme.

4 Add cavolo nero; stir until wilted. Remove pan from heat; stir through grated parmesan.

5 Serve risotto topped with flaked parmesan.

kale salad with creamy zucchini dressing

PREP + COOK TIME 25 MINUTES • SERVES 6

1 cup (200g) red or white quinoa

2 cups (500ml) water

200g (6½ ounces) purple kale, trimmed, washed, shredded finely

1 large carrot (180g), unpeeled, grated coarsely

1 cup (100g) walnuts, roasted, chopped coarsely

CREAMY ZUCCHINI DRESSING

2 small zucchini (180g), chopped coarsely

1 large avocado (320g), chopped coarsely

⅓ cup (35g) walnuts, roasted

1 clove garlic, crushed

2 tablespoons white wine vinegar

2 tablespoons walnut oil

2 tablespoons olive oil

1 Make creamy zucchini dressing.

2 Place quinoa and the water in a medium saucepan; bring to the boil. Reduce heat to low; simmer, covered, for 10 minutes or until tender. Drain; cool.

3 Place quinoa in a large bowl with kale, carrot, walnuts and dressing; toss gently to combine. Season to taste.

CREAMY ZUCCHINI DRESSING Process zucchini, avocado, walnuts, garlic and vinegar until smooth. With motor operating, gradually add oils, drop by drop, then in a slow steady stream, until thick and creamy. Season to taste.

Test Kitchen
NOTES

Quinoa and walnuts are packed with ample protein to make this a meal in itself, however you could serve it as a side dish with grilled chicken, fish or a poached egg. It would also make a delicious filling for wraps or a sandwich.

indian-spiced quinoa cakes with tomatoes

PREP + COOK TIME 50 MINUTES
(+ COOLING & REFRIGERATION) • SERVES 4

400g (12½ ounces) kumara (orange sweet potato), peeled, cut into 4cm (1½-inch) cubes

2 cups (500ml) water

1 cup (200g) white quinoa

⅓ cup (80ml) olive oil

1 medium onion (150g), chopped finely

2 cloves garlic, crushed

4cm (1½-inch) piece fresh ginger (20g), grated finely

1 fresh long red chilli, chopped finely

1½ tablespoons indian curry powder

⅓ cup chopped fresh coriander (cilantro)

1 egg

¼ cup (40g) wholemeal plain (all-purpose) flour

1 tablespoon olive oil, extra

500g (1 pound) ripe roma (egg) tomatoes, cut into wedges

1 tablespoon yellow mustard seeds

2 tablespoons fresh curry leaves

⅔ cup (190g) Greek-style yoghurt

2 cups (40g) baby asian salad leaves

1 Cook kumara in a medium saucepan of boiling water for 5 minutes or until tender. Drain well. Mash kumara. Cool.

2 Bring the water to the boil in a small saucepan. Stir in quinoa; cook, covered, over low heat for 15 minutes or until tender. Drain well. Cool.

3 Heat 1 tablespoon of the oil in a medium frying pan over medium heat; cook onion, stirring, for 8 minutes or until soft. Add garlic, ginger, chilli and curry powder; cook, stirring, over low heat for 3 minutes or until soft and fragrant.

4 Combine mashed kumara, quinoa and onion mixture in a large bowl with coriander, egg and flour; season. Form level ½-cups of the mixture into eight 8cm (3¼-inch) patties. Place on a baking-paper-lined tray. Cover; refrigerate 30 minutes or until chilled.

5 Heat remaining oil in a large frying pan over medium heat; cook patties, in batches, for 3 minutes each side or until golden and heated through. Drain on paper towel.

6 Heat extra oil in same pan over medium heat; cook tomato, seeds and curry leaves, stirring occasionally, for 5 minutes or until tomato is softened. Season to taste.

7 Serve quinoa cakes with tomato, yoghurt and salad leaves.

stuffed capsicums

PREP + COOK TIME 3 HOURS 45 MINUTES • MAKES 5

2 tablespoons olive oil

1 medium brown onion (150g), chopped finely

3 cloves garlic, crushed

2 tablespoons tomato paste

1 cup (280g) bottled passata

¾ cup (150g) quinoa

1 cup (250ml) chicken stock

400g (12½ ounces) canned brown lentils, rinsed, drained

180g (5½ ounces) greek fetta, crumbled

⅓ cup (50g) pitted black olives, finely chopped

¼ cup coarsely chopped fresh flat-leaf parsley

¼ cup coarsely chopped fresh basil

5 medium capsicums (1kg)

1 Heat oil in a large frying pan over medium heat; cook onion and garlic, stirring, for 5 minutes or until onion softens. Add paste, passata, quinoa and stock; bring to the boil. Remove from heat. Stir in lentils, fetta, olives and herbs. Season to taste.
2 Cut tops from each capsicum; reserve tops. Using a small spoon, scoop out membranes and seeds. Trim bases level so that capsicums stand upright. Divide quinoa mixture among capsicums; replace tops.
3 Place capsicums into a 4.5-litre (18-cup) slow cooker. Cook, covered, on high, about 3 hours.

roasted broccoli with barley and haloumi

1 cup (200g) pearl barley

850g (1¾ pounds) broccoli

3 cloves garlic, sliced thinly

2 fresh long red chillies, halved lengthways, seeded, sliced thinly

½ cup (125ml) extra virgin olive oil

180g (5½ ounces) haloumi cheese, cut into 1.5cm (¾-inch) slices

2 tablespoons lemon juice

1 cup loosely packed torn fresh mint leaves

1 cup coarsely chopped fresh coriander (cilantro) leaves

2 tablespoons dukkah

1 Preheat oven to 220°C/425°F.

2 Cook barley in a large saucepan of boiling salted water, uncovered, for 30 minutes or until tender; drain.

3 Meanwhile, cut broccoli into large florets. Combine broccoli, garlic, chilli and ¼ cup of the oil in a large shallow baking dish; season. Roast for 10 minutes or until broccoli is almost tender and beginning to brown. Add haloumi; roast a further 10 minutes or until haloumi is heated through and browned lightly.

4 Drizzle remaining oil and juice over broccoli mixture. Combine broccoli mixture with barley and herbs. Season to taste. Serve sprinkled with dukkah.

This recipe would also be delicious using cauliflower instead of broccoli, or a mixture of both.

rosemary and tomato barley risotto with mozzarella

PREP + COOK TIME 55 MINUTES • SERVES 4

1 tablespoon olive oil

1 small onion (80g), chopped finely

2 cloves garlic, crushed

1 medium red capsicum (bell pepper) (200g), chopped finely

1 tablespoon fresh rosemary, chopped finely

1½ cups (300g) pearl barley

1.25 litres (5 cups) vegetable stock

400g (12½ ounces) canned diced tomatoes

1 cup (280g) bottled passata

2 teaspoons caster (superfine) sugar

2 teaspoons finely grated lemon rind

200g (6½ ounces) buffalo mozzarella, torn

1 tablespoon chilli-infused olive oil

½ cup loosely packed fresh flat-leaf parsley leaves

1 Heat olive oil in a large saucepan over medium heat; cook onion, garlic, capsicum and rosemary for 5 minutes or until tender.

2 Add barley; cook, stirring, about 1 minute. Add stock, tomatoes, passata, sugar and rind; bring to the boil. Reduce heat to low; cook, stirring occasionally, for 45 minutes or until barley is tender. Season to taste.

3 Spoon risotto into bowls; top with mozzarella, drizzle with chilli oil and sprinkle with parsley.

Test Kitchen
NOTES

Passata is pureed and sieved Italian tomatoes and is available from supermarkets. Use a pinch of chilli flakes or chopped fresh chilli and extra virgin olive oil instead of chilli-infused oil. You could also use fresh cow's milk mozzarella, which is known as *fior di latte*, literally meaning 'flower of the milk'.

quinoa and seed cheese damper

PREP + COOK TIME 1 HOUR 5 MINUTES
(+ STANDING) • MAKES 12 SLICES

¼ cup (50g) red quinoa

½ cup (125ml) boiling water

3 cups (450g) self-raising flour

2 teaspoons sea salt

40g (1½ ounces) butter, chopped

¼ cup (50g) roasted buckwheat

2 tablespoons linseeds

2 tablespoons pepitas (pumpkin seed kernels)

¾ cup (90g) grated vintage cheddar

½ cup (125ml) milk

¾ cup (180ml) water, approximately

1 Place quinoa in a small heatproof bowl; cover with the boiling water. Stand 20 minutes. Drain well.

2 Preheat oven to 180°C/350°F. Flour a large oven tray.

3 Place flour and salt in a large bowl; rub in butter. Stir in quinoa, buckwheat, linseeds, pepitas and cheddar. Stir in milk and enough of the water to mix to a soft dough. Knead dough on a floured surface until smooth.

4 Place dough on tray; press into a 16cm (6½-inch) round. Brush with a little extra water or milk; sprinkle with a little extra flour. Cut a 1cm (½-inch) deep cross in top of dough.

5 Bake for 50 minutes or until golden brown and damper sounds hollow when tapped on the base.

barley and vegetable soup
with crunchy seeds

PREP + COOK TIME 45 MINUTES • SERVES 6

2 tablespoons extra virgin olive oil

1 large red onion (300g),
chopped into small pieces

1 medium parsnip (250g),
chopped into small pieces

2 stalks celery (300g), trimmed,
chopped into small pieces

4 cloves garlic, chopped finely

1 cup (280g) bottled passata

1 litre (4 cups) vegetable stock

1 litre (4 cups) water

2 medium red capsicums (bell peppers) (400g),
chopped into small pieces

400g (12½ ounces) canned cannellini beans,
rinsed, drained

½ cup (100g) pearl barley, rinsed, drained

2 tablespoons pepitas (pumpkin seeds)

2 tablespoons sunflower seeds

2 tablespoons rinsed, drained baby capers

2 tablespoons dried currants

¼ cup loosely packed torn fresh basil leaves

½ cup (40g) finely grated parmesan

1 Heat half the oil in a large saucepan over medium heat; cook onion, parsnip, celery and garlic, stirring, for 5 minutes or until vegetables have softened.

2 Add passata, stock and the water; bring to the boil. Stir in capsicum, beans and barley; simmer, covered, for 25 minutes or until barley is tender. Season to taste.

3 Meanwhile, heat remaining oil in a small frying pan over medium-high heat; cook seeds and capers, stirring, until browned lightly and fragrant. Add currants; stir until combined.

4 Just before serving, stir basil into soup. Ladle soup into serving bowls; sprinkle with seed mixture and parmesan.

This soup, without the seed
topping, can be frozen
for up to 3 months.

Test Kitchen
NOTES

This salad of grains, nuts and fruit can be eaten as a light lunch or served as a side dish with chicken or lamb. Swap cherries for grapes.

chickpea, barley, orange and cherry salad

PREP + COOK TIME 45 MINUTES (+ STANDING) • SERVES 4

You will need to soak the barley in cold water for 3 hours before you start this recipe. Drain barley before cooking.

1½ cups (300g) pearl barley

500g (1 pound) butternut pumpkin, cut into 1.5cm (¾-inch) pieces

1 tablespoon olive oil

2 teaspoons cumin seeds

2 medium oranges (480g)

400g (12½ ounces) canned chickpeas (garbanzo beans), rinsed, drained

⅓ cup (55g) almonds, roasted, chopped coarsely

¼ cup (35g) sunflower seeds, toasted lightly

300g (9½ ounces) cherries, halved, pitted

¼ cup chopped fresh mint

2 tablespoons chopped fresh flat-leaf parsley

2 tablespoons pomegranate molasses

½ cup (125ml) extra virgin olive oil

2 tablespoon small fresh mint leaves, extra

1 Preheat oven to 220°C/425°F.

2 Cook soaked barley in a large saucepan of boiling water for 25 minutes or until tender; drain. Rinse under cold water; drain well.

3 Meanwhile, combine pumpkin, olive oil and cumin seeds on a large oven tray; season. Bake for 20 minutes or until tender and beginning to brown around edges.

4 Remove rind from oranges into long thin strips. Segment oranges over a bowl to catch the juice (see cooking techniques on page 112); reserve 2 tablespoons of the juice.

5 Place barley, pumpkin, orange segments and rind in a large bowl with chickpeas, almonds, seeds, cherries and herbs. Combine reserved juice, pomegranate molasses and extra virgin olive oil in a small jug. Drizzle dressing over salad, season to taste; toss gently to combine. Serve salad topped with extra mint.

quinoa, zucchini and fetta salad

PREP + COOK TIME 25 MINUTES (+ COOLING) · SERVES 4

¾ cup (150g) white quinoa

1½ cups (375ml) water

½ cup (70g) hazelnuts

2 medium zucchini (240g), cut into long thin strips

250g (8 ounces) heirloom or mixed cherry tomatoes, halved

½ small red onion (50g), sliced thinly

100g (3 ounces) fetta, crumbled

1 cup loosely packed fresh small basil leaves

2 tablespoons extra virgin olive oil

1 tablespoon red wine vinegar

1 Rinse quinoa under cold water; drain well. Place in a medium saucepan with the water; bring to the boil. Reduce heat; simmer, covered, for 15 minutes or until water is absorbed and quinoa is tender. Transfer to a large serving bowl to cool.

2 Meanwhile, roast hazelnuts in a medium frying pan over medium heat for 4 minutes or until golden. Rub hot hazelnuts in a clean tea towel to remove most of the skin; discard skin. Coarsely chop nuts.

3 Add nuts to quinoa in bowl with zucchini, tomato, onion, half the fetta and half the basil. Drizzle with combined oil and vinegar; toss gently to combine. Season to taste. Serve topped with remaining fetta and basil.

Test Kitchen NOTES

Serve with a green salad or steamed asparagus and crusty bread. Use a mandoline or V-slicer for the zucchini or coarsely grate it, if you like.

quinoa salad with char-grilled vegetables and tuna

PREP + COOK TIME 25 MINUTES • SERVES 4

1 large red capsicum (bell pepper) (350g), quartered

2 medium zucchini (240g), sliced thinly

2 baby eggplant (1200g), sliced thinly

1 medium red onion (170g), cut into wedges

⅔ cup (140g) quinoa, rinsed, drained

1⅓ cups (330ml) water

1 tablespoon olive oil

⅓ cup (80ml) lemon juice

2 teaspoons dijon mustard

2 x 185g (6½ ounces) canned tuna in springwater, drained

¼ cup baby basil leaves

1 Cook capsicum, zucchini, eggplant and onion on a heated oiled grill plate (or grill or barbecue) until tender. Slice capsicum thickly.

2 Meanwhile, place quinoa in a medium saucepan with the water; bring to the boil. Reduce heat to low; simmer, covered, for 15 minutes or until tender and water is absorbed. Remove from heat; stand 10 minutes, then fluff with a fork.

3 Combine oil, juice and mustard in a screw-top jar; shake well.

4 Place quinoa, vegetables and tuna in a bowl with dressing; toss gently to combine. Serve topped with basil.

Test Kitchen
NOTES

You could also use fresh mint or coriander. The salad tastes just as good at room temperature, so any leftovers will make a great packed lunch.

pearl barley salad

1 large beetroot (beet) (200g), peeled, cut into wedges

1 medium brown onion, cut into wedges

2 teaspoons olive oil

200g broccoli florets

½ cup (100g) pearl barley

1 tablespoon tahini

1 tablespoon warm water

1 tablespoon lemon juice

½ cup fresh flat-leaf parsley leaves

1 Preheat oven to 220°C/425°F.

2 Place beetroot and onion on a large oven tray; drizzle with oil. Roast about 20 minutes. Add broccoli; roast a further 15 minutes or until golden and tender.

3 Cook barley in a medium saucepan of boiling water for 40 minutes or until tender; drain well.

4 Meanwhile, combine tahini, the warm water and juice in a small bowl.

5 Toss roasted vegetables and parsley through warm barley. Drizzle with tahini dressing to serve.

green barley salad

PREP + COOK TIME 30 MINUTES • SERVES 6

1 cup (200g) pearl barley

1 cup (120g) frozen peas

1 cup (150g) shelled edamame

150g (4½ ounces) snow peas, sliced thinly

2 green onions (scallions), chopped finely

½ cup loosely packed fresh mint leaves

2 tablespoons extra virgin olive oil

1 tablespoon lemon juice

335g (10½ ounces) labne in olive oil, drained

1 Cook barley in a medium saucepan of salted water over medium heat for 25 minutes or until tender. Drain; rinse under cold water until cold, drain well.

2 Meanwhile, bring a medium saucepan of salted water to the boil. Add peas, edamame and snow peas; boil about 1 minute. Drain; place in a bowl of iced water until cold. Drain well.

3 Place barley and pea mixture in a shallow serving dish with onion and mint; drizzle with combined oil and juice. Toss gently to combine. Season to taste.

4 Serve salad topped with labne.

barley with pistachio and green olives

PREP + COOK TIME 30 MINUTES • SERVES 4

1½ cups (300g) pearl barley

4 large pitta bread (320g)

¾ cup (210g) Greek-style yoghurt

1 teaspoon finely grated lemon rind

1 cup loosely packed fresh mint leaves, chopped finely

2 cups (280g) green (sicilian) olives

¾ cup (100g) shelled pistachios

¼ radicchio (80g), shredded finely

1 long green chilli, chopped finely

¼ cup (60ml) lemon juice

2 tablespoons olive oil

1 Cook barley in a medium saucepan of boiling water for 20 minutes or until tender; drain.

2 Heat a grill plate (or grill or barbecue); cook bread until toasted lightly on both sides.

3 Meanwhile, combine yoghurt, rind and 2 teaspoons of the mint in a small bowl.

4 Place barley in a large bowl with olives, pistachios, radicchio, chilli, juice, oil and remaining mint; toss gently to combine. Season to taste. Serve with toasted bread, minted yoghurt and extra mint leaves, if you like.

4 ways with
PORRIDGE

pear and almond rice porridge

PREP + COOK TIME 15 MINUTES • **SERVES** 2

Combine ¾ cup rolled rice, 1 cup each water and rice milk and ¼ teaspoon ground cinnamon in a small saucepan; cook, covered, stirring occasionally, until mixture comes to the boil. Reduce heat; simmer, covered, stirring occasionally, for 5 minutes or until rice is soft. Remove from heat; stand, covered, 5 minutes. Stir 2 tablespoons almond kernels in a heated small frying pan until browned lightly; remove from heat, chop coarsely. Thinly slice 1 small unpeeled pear on a mandoline or V-slicer. Serve porridge sprinkled with almonds and 1 tablespoon LSA. Top with pear and drizzle with 1 teaspoon honey.

berry semolina porridge

PREP + COOK TIME 10 MINUTES • **SERVES** 2

Combine 1 cup milk, ½ cup water, 1 teaspoon vanilla extract and pinch ground cinnamon in a medium saucepan. Bring to the boil. Gradually add ⅓ cup semolina. Whisk over medium heat for 2 minutes or until thick. Remove from heat; stir in ⅔ cup thawed mixed berries. Divide porridge into serving bowls. Top with ¼ cup Greek-style yoghurt, 2 tablespoons chopped raw pistachios, 2 teaspoons honey and ⅓ cup extra berries.

test kitchen notes

Use your favourite nuts in this recipe to add crunch and fibre.

quinoa porridge with figs and raspberries

PREP + COOK TIME 25 MINUTES • SERVES 4

Place 1 cup rinsed, drained white quinoa and 3 cups water in a large saucepan; bring to the boil. Reduce heat to low; cook, covered, for 15 minutes or until quinoa is almost tender and water is absorbed. Add ½ cup milk, 2 tablespoons brown sugar and 1 teaspoon ground cinnamon; stir to combine. Cook for 5 minutes or until tender. Cut 2 fresh large figs into wedges. Serve porridge topped with figs and 150g (4½ ounces) fresh raspberries; drizzle with honey.

test kitchen notes

You can use red or black quinoa for a bit of colour; the cooking time will remain the same.

quinoa porridge with grapes and pistachios

PREP + COOK TIME 25 MINUTES • SERVES 4

Place 1 cup rinsed, drained white quinoa and 3 cups water in a large saucepan; bring to the boil. Reduce heat to low; cook, covered, about 10 minutes. Add 1 cup milk; cook, covered, a further 5 minutes or until quinoa is tender. Stir in 2 medium coarsely grated pink lady apples and 100g (3 ounces) halved seedless red grapes. Serve porridge topped with another 100g halved seedless red grapes and ⅓ cup coarsely chopped toasted pistachios; drizzle with 2 tablespoons honey.

test kitchen notes

Most quinoa comes rinsed, but it's a good habit to rinse it yourself under cold water until the water runs clear, then drain it. This removes any remaining outer coating.

wheat and spelt

spelt pizza with kumara, pepitas and goat's cheese

PREP + COOK TIME 1 HOUR 20 MINUTES (+ STANDING) • SERVES 4

2 teaspoons (7g) dried yeast

½ teaspoon salt

2 cups (320g) plain (all-purpose) spelt flour

1 cup (250ml) warm water

⅓ cup (80ml) olive oil

3 medium onions (600g), halved, sliced thinly

2 cloves garlic, crushed

800g (1½ pounds) kumara (orange sweet potato), sliced thinly

⅓ cup (65g) pepitas (pumpkin seeds)

1 fresh long green chilli, seeded, chopped finely

200g (7 ounces) soft goat's cheese, crumbled

20g (¾ ounce) baby rocket (arugula)

1 Combine yeast, salt and flour in a large bowl; make a well in the centre. Stir in the warm water and 2 tablespoons of the oil until mixed well. Knead dough on a floured surface for 5 minutes or until smooth and elastic. Place dough in an oiled bowl; cover with plastic wrap. Stand 30 minutes or until doubled in size.

2 Heat remaining oil in a large frying pan over medium-high heat; cook onion and garlic, stirring occasionally, about 5 minutes. Reduce heat to low; cook, stirring occasionally, for 20 minutes or until onion is light golden. Cool.

3 Preheat oven to 220°C/425°F. Oil two 30cm (12-inch) pizza trays.

4 Divide dough in half, roll each half to a 25cm (10-inch) round; place on tray. Spread onion mixture between pizza bases; top with kumara, slightly overlapping the slices, and pepitas.

5 Bake pizzas for 15 minutes, swapping trays halfway through cooking time, or until crust is golden. Serve topped with chilli, goat's cheese and rocket.

Test Kitchen
NOTES

For extra protein, add
2 tablespoons chia seeds
to the pizza dough. Use
a mandoline or V-slicer
to easily cut the kumara
into thin slices.

spiced chickpea and cauliflower dosa

PREP + COOK TIME 45 MINUTES • MAKES 6

2 tablespoons vegetable oil

1 large onion (200g), chopped finely

2 cloves garlic, crushed

2 teaspoons cumin seeds

1 tablespoon finely grated fresh ginger

1 tablespoon indian curry powder

2 teaspoons yellow mustard seeds

500g (1 pound) cauliflower, cut into small florets

400g (12½ ounces) canned chickpeas (garbanzo beans), rinsed, drained

1 cup (250ml) vegetable stock

1½ tablespoons vegetable oil, extra

½ cup loosely packed fresh coriander (cilantro) leaves

3 limes, halved

CUCUMBER YOGHURT

1 cup (280g) Greek-style yoghurt

1 lebanese cucumber (130g), grated coarsely

1 teaspoon dried mint

DOSA BATTER

1 cup (150g) chickpea flour (besan)

1 cup (150g) plain (all-purpose) flour

1 teaspoon ground cumin

½ teaspoon bicarbonate of soda (baking soda)

¼ teaspoon sea salt flakes

2 cups (500ml) cold water

1 Heat oil in a large frying pan over medium heat; cook onion, garlic, cumin seeds, ginger, curry powder and mustard seeds for 5 minutes or until onion is soft. Add cauliflower and chickpeas; cook stirring, about 2 minutes. Add stock; cook, partially covered, for 15 minutes or until cauliflower is tender. Roughly mash cauliflower and chickpeas with the back of a spoon. Season to taste. Set aside; keep warm.

2 Make cucumber yoghurt.

3 Make dosa batter.

4 Heat 1 teaspoon of the extra oil in a 25cm (10-inch) frying pan over medium heat. Add ½ cup of the dosa batter and quickly spread with a metal spatula to cover the base; cook for 2 minutes or until mixture bubbles. Top with one-sixth of the cauliflower mixture; cook a further 2 minutes or until base is crisp and golden. Roll up dosa to enclose filling; slide onto a plate. Repeat with remaining oil, batter and cauliflower mixture to make six in total.

5 Serve dosa scattered with coriander, accompany with cucumber yoghurt and lime.

CUCUMBER YOGHURT Combine ingredients in a medium bowl. Season to taste.

DOSA BATTER Sift flours, cumin, bicarbonate of soda and salt into a bowl. Whisk in the cold water until combined.

seeded pumpkin bread

PREP + COOK TIME 2 HOURS 30 MINUTES (+ STANDING) • MAKES 8 SLICES

900g (1¼-pound) butternut pumpkin, halved lengthways, seeds removed

2 teaspoons (7g) dried yeast

1 tablespoon honey

½ cup (125ml) lukewarm water

2 tablespoons vegetable oil

1⅓ cups (200g) wholemeal plain (all-purpose) flour

2 cups (300g) '00' flour, bread flour or plain (all-purpose) flour

½ cup (75g) sunflower seeds

2 tablespoons sesame seeds

1 tablespoon linseeds

1 tablespoon sea salt flakes

1 egg, beaten lightly

2 tablespoons pepitas (pumpkin seeds)

2 teaspoons poppy seeds

1 Preheat oven to 180°C/350°F.

2 Place pumpkin on an oven tray, cover with foil; bake for 1¼ hours or until very tender. When cool enough to handle, scoop flesh into a medium bowl; mash with a fork.

3 Meanwhile, combine yeast, honey and the lukewarm water in a small bowl; cover with plastic wrap. Stand in a warm place for 10 minutes or until frothy. Stir in oil.

4 Combine flours, seeds and salt in a large bowl. Add yeast mixture and mashed pumpkin; mix to a soft dough. Knead dough on a floured surface for 10 minutes or until smooth and elastic. Place dough in a large oiled bowl; cover with plastic wrap. Stand in a warm place for 1 hour or until doubled in size.

5 Increase oven to 220°C/425°F. Punch down the dough with your fist. Knead on a floured surface for 1 minute or until smooth. Shape dough into a 20cm (8-inch) round; place on a large oiled oven tray. Cover loosely with oiled plastic wrap. Stand in a warm place 40 minutes or until almost doubled in size.

6 Brush dough with egg, sprinkle with pepitas and poppy seeds. Using a sharp, thin-bladed knife, make five shallow cuts across the top of the dough. Bake about 20 minutes. Reduce oven to 180°C/350°F; bake a further 10 minutes or until golden and bread sounds hollow when tapped. Cool on a wire rack.

Test Kitchen
NOTES

You will need 1½ cups
mashed pumpkin. If you
have an electric mixer
with a dough hook, knead
dough on medium speed
for 6 minutes or until
smooth and elastic.

roast beetroot, garlic and chia seed tart

PREP + COOK TIME 1 HOUR 15 MINUTES
(+ STANDING & REFRIGERATION) • SERVES 4

500g (1 pound) baby beetroot (beets), stems and leaves attached

8 cloves garlic, unpeeled

6 sprigs fresh thyme

2½ tablespoons olive oil

3 medium red onions (510g), sliced thinly

60g (2 ounces) soft goat's cheese, crumbled

1 clove garlic, crushed, extra

2 tablespoons extra virgin olive oil

2 tablespoons orange juice

1 teaspoon white chia seeds

PASTRY

2 tablespoons white chia seeds

2 tablespoons warm water

1½ cups (240g) wholemeal plain (all-purpose) flour

1 teaspoon sea salt flakes

50g (1½ ounces) cold unsalted butter, chopped

1 egg

¼ cup (60ml) olive oil

1 Trim beetroot, leaving a little of the stems attached. Finely chop enough of the beetroot stems to make 2 tablespoons; reserve for the pastry. Pick 20g (¾ ounce) small beetroot leaves, cover with a damp paper towel; refrigerate until ready to use. Pick a further 100g (3 ounces) beetroot leaves, shred finely; refrigerate. Discard remaining stems and leaves.

2 Make pastry.

3 Preheat oven to 200°C/400°F. Line an oven tray with foil.

4 Place beetroot, garlic and thyme in centre of tray; drizzle with 2 teaspoons of the olive oil. Wrap foil around beetroot. Roast about 20 minutes; check garlic, remove if tender when lightly squeezed. Roast beetroot a further 10 minutes or until tender; discard thyme. Peel beetroot; cut into quarters.

5 Meanwhile, heat remaining olive oil in a large frying pan over low heat; cook onions, stirring occasionally, for 20 minutes or until very soft. Add shredded beetroot leaves; stir for 3 minutes or until wilted. Season to taste. Cool.

6 Roll pastry between sheets of baking paper into a 30cm (12-inch) round. Using a bowl as a guide, trim pastry into a 29cm (11¾-inch) round. Fold in the edge to create a 1cm (½-inch) border.

7 Slide pastry with the paper onto a large oven tray; bake for 12 minutes or until golden. Spread onion mixture on tart base; top with roasted beetroot and garlic and goat's cheese. Bake a further 10 minutes or until cheese is golden.

8 Whisk extra garlic, extra virgin olive oil and juice together in a small bowl; season to taste. Add small beetroot leaves; toss to coat. Top tart with beetroot leaves; sprinkle with chia seeds.

PASTRY Combine chia seeds and the warm water in a medium bowl; stand 20 minutes. Add flour, salt and butter; rub together until mixture resembles coarse crumbs. Stir in reserved beetroot stems. Whisk egg and oil in a small bowl, add to flour mixture; mix with your hands until just combined. Shape pastry into a disc. Cover; refrigerate 30 minutes.

spinach and broccolini pasta with rocket and walnut pesto

PREP + COOK TIME 35 MINUTES • SERVES 6

400g (12½ ounces) wholemeal spaghetti

470g (15 ounces) broccolini, trimmed, cut into 4cm (1½-inch) lengths

2 tablespoons olive oil

2 cloves garlic, crushed

400g (12½ ounces) baby spinach leaves

1 cup (240g) ricotta, crumbled

½ cup (50g) walnuts, roasted, chopped coarsely

ROCKET AND WALNUT PESTO

60g (2 ounces) rocket (arugula) leaves

1 cup firmly packed fresh basil leaves

½ cup (50g) walnuts, roasted

2 cloves garlic, crushed

1 teaspoon finely grated lemon rind

⅓ cup (25g) finely grated parmesan

½ cup (125ml) extra virgin olive oil

1 Make rocket and walnut pesto.

2 Cook pasta in a large saucepan of boiling salted water for 10 minutes or until almost tender, adding broccolini in last 2 minutes of cooking. Drain well; reserve ½ cup of the cooking water.

3 Meanwhile, heat oil in a large saucepan over medium heat; cook garlic and spinach, stirring occasionally, for 2 minutes or until just wilted. Season. Add pasta, broccolini, pesto and enough reserved cooking water to combine the sauce.

4 Serve pasta topped with ricotta and walnuts.

ROCKET AND WALNUT PESTO Process rocket, basil, walnuts, garlic, rind, parmesan and 1 tablespoon of the oil until roughly chopped. With motor operating, add remaining oil in a thin, steady stream until mixture is smooth. Season to taste.

Test Kitchen
NOTES

It's a good idea to remove the thin paper skins from the walnuts after roasting as they can add a slight bitterness to the pesto. While the nuts are still warm, rub them together in a clean tea towel to remove most of the skins. If you like, you can use almonds instead of the walnuts in the pesto.

spelt pasta with braised capsicum, nuts and chilli

PREP + COOK TIME 50 MINUTES • SERVES 4

¼ cup (60ml) olive oil

1 medium onion (150g), chopped finely

2 cloves garlic, crushed

1 teaspoon fennel seeds

3 medium red capsicums (bell peppers) (600g), diced

3 medium yellow capsicums (bell peppers) (600g), diced

1 fresh long red chilli, seeded, chopped finely

2 tablespoons tomato paste

1¾ cups (430ml) vegetable stock

2 tablespoons red wine vinegar

375g (12 ounces) spelt fettuccine

1 cup fresh basil leaves

2 tablespoons pine nuts, toasted

½ cup (40g) shaved parmesan

1 Heat oil in a large saucepan over medium-high heat; cook onion, garlic and fennel seeds, stirring about 5 minutes. Add capsicums and chilli; cook, covered, stirring occasionally, about 8 minutes. Stir in paste; cook about 2 minutes. Add stock; bring to the boil. Reduce heat; simmer, covered, for 25 minutes or until capsicum is very tender. Remove from heat; stir in vinegar. Season to taste.

2 Meanwhile, cook pasta in a large saucepan of salted water until almost tender; drain. Return pasta to the pan.

3 Add capsicum mixture to pasta with half the basil; toss to combine. Serve pasta in bowls topped with pine nuts, parmesan and remaining basil.

pasta with almond and walnut paste, pears and broad beans

PREP + COOK TIME 25 MINUTES • SERVES 4

½ cup (80g) almonds, roasted

½ cup (50g) walnuts, roasted

2 cloves garlic, crushed

¼ cup firmly packed watercress sprigs

½ teaspoon freshly ground black pepper

½ cup (125ml) extra virgin olive oil

400g (12½ ounces) spelt penne

2 medium pears (460g), unpeeled, cored, cut into eight wedges

1 tablespoon olive oil

2 cups (240g) frozen broad (fava) beans, blanched, peeled

1½ cups firmly packed watercress sprigs, extra

⅓ cup (25g) shaved pecorino or parmesan

1 Process nuts, garlic, watercress and pepper until finely chopped. With motor operating, gradually pour in ¼ cup of the extra virgin olive oil until combined. Season with salt to taste.

2 Cook pasta in a large saucepan of boiling salted water for 8 minutes or until almost tender. Drain; reserve ½ cup of the cooking water. Return pasta to pan; cover to keep warm.

3 Meanwhile, season pears. Heat olive oil in a large frying pan over medium heat; cook pears for 2 minutes each side or until golden. Drain on paper towel.

4 Add nut paste to pasta with enough reserved cooking water for paste to coat pasta (do not return the pan to the heat or the paste will thicken and make the mixture dry). Add pear, broad beans and extra watercress; toss gently to combine. Season to taste.

5 Serve pasta topped with cheese, drizzled with remaining extra virgin olive oil.

Test Kitchen NOTES

The nut paste can be made a day ahead; store in an airtight container in the fridge until ready to use. We've left the skin on the pears in this recipe; any bitterness from the skin and pepperiness from the watercress is easily balanced by the sweetness of the pear flesh.

Test Kitchen
NOTES

Clams need to be soaked in salted water first to purge them of any sand. You can use wholemeal spaghetti instead of the spelt spaghetti, if you like. If you are a chilli fan, simply add 1 fresh long finely chopped red chilli with the onion in step 4.

spelt spaghetti with cherry tomato sauce and vongole

You will need to soak the vongole (clams) in salted water for 30 minutes before you start this recipe.

1 bunch fresh basil (80g)

950g (2 pounds) heirloom cherry tomatoes, halved

1 medium lemon (140g), cut into 8 wedges

¼ cup (60ml) olive oil

375g (12 ounces) spelt spaghetti

1 medium red onion (170g), chopped finely

3 cloves garlic, sliced thinly

1kg (2 pounds) vongole (clams)

¾ cup (180ml) dry white wine

1 Preheat oven to 200°C/400°F.

2 Pick leaves from basil; reserve 1 cup of the smallest leaves. Tie basil stalks together with kitchen string. Place in a baking dish with tomato, lemon and 2 tablespoons of the oil; season, then toss to coat. Roast for 15 minutes or until tomato softens. Discard basil stalks. Squeeze juice from lemon over tomato; discard lemon. Mash half the tomato with a fork.

3 Meanwhile, cook pasta in a large saucepan of boiling water until almost tender.

4 Heat remaining oil in a large, deep frying pan over medium-high heat; cook onion and garlic, stirring, for 5 minutes or until softened. Add vongole and wine; boil, stirring, about 1 minute. Cook, covered, for 5 minutes or until vongole just open. Add tomato mixture, pasta and ¾ cup of the reserved basil leaves, then season; toss to combine.

5 Serve in bowls topped with remaining basil leaves.

primavera soup with pangrattato

30g (1 ounce) butter

4 shallots (100g), chopped

1 litre (4 cups) vegetable stock

2 cups (500ml) water

⅓ cup (75g) risoni pasta

250g (8 ounces) baby green zucchini, halved lengthways

150g (4½ ounces) asparagus, cut into 3cm (1¼-inch) lengths

2 cups (240g) frozen baby peas

PANGRATTATO

200g (6½ ounces) crusty italian bread

2 tablespoons extra virgin olive oil

1 fresh long red chilli, sliced thinly

2 cloves garlic, chopped

⅓ cup loosely packed small fresh flat-leaf parsley leaves

1 teaspoon finely grated lemon rind

1 Heat butter in a large saucepan over medium heat; cook shallots, stirring, for 3 minutes or until soft.
2 Add stock and the water to pan; bring to the boil. Add pasta and zucchini; simmer, uncovered, about 5 minutes, stirring occasionally.
3 Meanwhile, make pangrattato.
4 Add asparagus and peas to soup; simmer, uncovered, for 5 minutes or until just tender. Season to taste.
5 Ladle soup into serving bowls; top with pangrattato.

PANGRATTATO Remove crust from bread; tear into 1cm (½-inch) pieces. Heat oil in a large frying pan over medium-high heat; cook chilli and bread pieces, stirring, until browned lightly and crisp. Add garlic; cook until fragrant. Remove from heat; stir in parsley and rind. Season to taste.

Test Kitchen
NOTES

Swap baby zucchini for
thinly sliced zucchini.
This soup is best made
just before serving as it
will discolour on standing.

vegie curry pies

1 tablespoon vegetable oil

1 medium brown onion (150g), sliced

2 tablespoons panang curry paste

1 cup (250ml) coconut milk

2 baby (finger) eggplants (120g), peeled, sliced

1 medium desiree potato (200g), cut into 1.5cm (¾-inch) cubes

1 small kumara (orange sweet potato) (250g), cut into 1.5cm (¾-inch) cubes

1 tablespoon lime juice

1 teaspoon sesame oil

½ cup (75g) coarsely chopped roasted cashews

1 cup (120g) frozen peas

2 sheets puff pastry

1 egg, beaten lightly

1 Preheat oven to 200°C/400°F.

2 Heat vegetable oil in a medium saucepan or wok over medium-high heat; cook onion, stirring, for 3 minutes or until softened. Add paste; cook a further 2 minutes or until fragrant. Stir in coconut milk; bring to a simmer. Add eggplant, potato and kumara; cook, covered, for 10 minutes or until vegetables are tender. Remove from heat; stir in juice, sesame oil, cashews and peas; season to taste. Spread mixture in a shallow tray; cool in freezer 5 minutes.

3 Meanwhile, using a 1 cup (250ml) ramekin as a guide, cut four rounds from pastry, 2cm (¾ inch) larger than the dish.

4 Spoon curry mixture evenly into four ramekins. Lightly brush outer rims of ramekins with a little egg; cover with pastry lids, pressing overhanging pastry against sides. Brush pastry with a little more egg. Cut a small slit in the top of each pie. Place pies on an oven tray.

5 Bake for 15 minutes or until golden.

Serve with a tomato, onion and coriander
sambal or a mixed leaf salad.

dhal-stuffed paratha with raita

PREP + COOK TIME 1 HOUR (+ COOLING & REFRIGERATION) · SERVES 4

60g (2 ounces) ghee (clarified butter), melted

1 teaspoon garam masala

2 teaspoons ground ginger

½ teaspoon ground coriander

1 clove garlic, crushed

1 long green chilli, chopped finely

1 large sprig coriander (cilantro) with root

400g (12½ ounces) canned brown lentils, rinsed, drained

1 cup (250ml) water

½ cup (60g) frozen peas

2½ cups (375g) atta or wholemeal plain (all-purpose) flour

¾ cup (180ml) water, approximately, extra

RAITA

200g (6½ ounces) Greek-style yoghurt

1 tablespoon lemon juice

2 tablespoons water

1 tablespoon finely chopped mint

Swap ghee for 60ml vegetable oil. Atta is available from most major supermarkets and Indian food stores.

1 Heat 20g of the ghee in a large saucepan over medium heat; cook spices and garlic for 1 minute or until fragrant. Stir in chilli and chopped coriander root, then lentils and the water; bring to the boil. Reduce heat; simmer, uncovered, for 15 minutes or until lentils have broken down and absorbed the water.

2 Add peas to pan; cook for 2 minutes or until heated through. Stir in chopped coriander leaves and stem; season to taste. Remove from heat; refrigerate until cooled.

3 Meanwhile, combine flour and 20g of the ghee in a large bowl with enough of the extra water to form a firm dough. Knead dough for 5 minutes on a floured surface until smooth and elastic. Divide dough into four portions; place in a large bowl. Cover with plastic wrap.

4 Preheat oven to 120°C/250°F.

5 Roll out a portion of dough on a floured surface until 5mm (¼-inch) thick. Place a quarter of the cooled dhal mixture in the centre of the round; fold dough like a parcel to enclose filling. Using a rolling pin, gently roll paratha until 5mm (¼-inch) thick, taking care not to break the dough.

6 Heat 1 teaspoon of the remaining ghee in a non-stick frying pan over medium heat; cook paratha for 4 minutes each side or until golden. Transfer to an oven tray; keep warm in oven. Repeat with remaining dough, filling and ghee.

7 Meanwhile, make raita.

8 Serve paratha with raita; top with extra mint and coriander leaves, if you like.

RAITA Combine ingredients in a small bowl.

dried fig and walnut bread

PREP + COOK TIME 1 HOUR (+ STANDING & COOLING) • MAKES 15 SLICES

2 teaspoons (7g) dry yeast

2 teaspoons caster (superfine) sugar

1¼ cups (310ml) lukewarm water

3⅓ cups (500g) '00' flour, bread flour or plain (all-purpose) flour

2 teaspoons sea salt flakes (10g)

½ cup (55g) coarsely chopped walnuts

¾ cup (140g) coarsely chopped dried figs

Test Kitchen NOTES

If you don't have an electric mixer with a dough hook, knead the dough by hand on a lightly floured surface for 10 minutes by pulling and stretching every quarter turn. This bread is best made on the day of serving, but is also delicious toasted and served with cheese or spread with ricotta and drizzled with honey.

1 Combine yeast, sugar and the lukewarm water in a medium bowl of an electric mixer. Stand in a warm place 10 minutes or until bubbly.

2 Add flour and salt to bowl; mix with the dough hook on the knead setting for 5 minutes or until smooth and elastic. Transfer dough to a board; press out to flatten slightly. Top with walnuts and figs, knead into dough.

3 Place dough in an oiled bowl. Place bowl in a large plastic bag; seal bag. Stand in a warm place 45 minutes or until dough doubles in size.

4 Preheat oven to 220°C/425°F; heat an oven tray.

5 Punch down dough with fist. Knead dough on a floured surface into an oval shape, 28cm (11¼ inches) long. Place dough on a large piece of baking paper, then on a board. Place board in plastic bag; seal bag. Stand in a warm place 15 minutes or until risen slightly.

6 Remove bag; transfer dough to hot oven tray. Sprinkle the top with a little extra flour. Using a small sharp knife, make a shallow cut along the length of the loaf, leaving a 4cm (1½-inch) border at each end. Spray bread and tray lightly with a fine mist of water or sprinkle lightly with water.

7 Bake for 35 minutes or until browned and bread sounds hollow when tapped on the base. Transfer to a wire rack to cool.

4 ways with
PASTA

penne pesto

PREP + COOK TIME 15 MINUTES • **SERVES** 4

Cook 375g (12 ounces) penne in a large saucepan of boiling water until tender; drain, reserving ¼ cup of the cooking water. Combine pasta with ½ cup bottled pesto, 25g (¾ ounce) shaved parmesan and enough reserved cooking water to coat. Season to taste. Serve topped with basil leaves.

penne with chilli, garlic and oil

PREP + COOK TIME 15 MINUTES • **SERVES** 4

Cook 375g (12 ounces) penne in a large saucepan of boiling water until tender; drain, reserve ¼ cup of the cooking water. Heat 2 tablespoons olive oil in a medium frying pan over low heat; cook 1 large finely chopped red chilli, 1 clove crushed garlic and 1 tablespoon fresh oregano leaves, stirring, for 2 minutes or until chilli softens. Add pasta, 3 teaspoons lemon juice and enough reserved cooking water to coat with chilli mixture. Serve topped with ⅓ cup shaved parmesan, season to taste.

penne arrabbiata

PREP + COOK TIME 20 MINUTES • **SERVES** 4

Heat 1 tablespoon olive oil in a frying pan over low heat; cook 2 small finely chopped red thai chillies, 2 cloves crushed garlic and 4 torn fresh basil leaves, stirring for 2 minutes or until chilli softens. Add 400g (12½ ounces) canned crushed tomatoes; increase heat to medium, simmer for 10 minutes or until thickened slightly. Season. Meanwhile, cook 375g (12 ounces) penne in a large saucepan of boiling water until tender; drain, reserving ¼ cup of the cooking water. Stir pasta and 2 tablespoons coarsely grated parmesan into tomato mixture. Add enough reserved cooking water to coat the pasta. Serve topped with 2 tablespoons grated parmesan and 1 tablespoon small fresh basil leaves.

pumpkin and sage penne

PREP + COOK TIME 20 MINUTES • **SERVES** 4

Cook 375g (12 ounces) penne in a large saucepan of boiling water until tender; drain, reserve ¼ cup of the cooking water. Meanwhile, heat 1 tablespoon olive oil in a medium saucepan over medium heat; cook 1 clove crushed garlic and 7 fresh sage leaves, stirring, for 1 minute or until fragrant. Add 505g (1 pound) canned pumpkin soup, simmer, stirring occasionally, for 10 minutes or until thickened slightly. Stir through ½ cup coarsely grated vintage cheddar. Stir pasta into pumpkin mixture with enough reserved cooking water to coat. Season to taste. Top with 2 tablespoons extra coarsely grated vintage cheddar. Serve topped with extra sage leaves fried in oil until crisp.

corn

corn soup with parmesan crisps and chilli

8 trimmed corn cobs (2kg)

30g (1 ounce) butter

1 large brown onion (200g), chopped finely

2 cups (500ml) vegetable stock

1 cup (250ml) water

1 cup (250ml) thickened (heavy) cream

1 tablespoon vegetable oil

1 fresh long red chilli, sliced thinly

⅔ cup (10g) puffed corn

½ cup fresh baby coriander (cilantro) leaves

PARMESAN CRISPS

⅓ cup (25g) finely grated parmesan

1 Cut kernels from corn cobs.

2 Heat butter in a large saucepan over medium heat; cook onion, stirring, until soft but not coloured. Add stock and the water; bring to the boil. Add corn kernels; simmer, covered, for 20 minutes or until corn is tender. Stand 10 minutes.

3 Meanwhile, make parmesan crisps.

4 Blend half the soup mixture until smooth; return to pan. Stir in cream over medium heat until hot. Season to taste.

5 Heat oil in a small frying pan; cook chilli, stirring, until soft.

6 Ladle soup into serving bowls; top with puffed corn, chilli and the oil, then coriander. Serve with parmesan crisps.

PARMESAN CRISPS Preheat oven to 180°C/350°F. Line a large oven tray with baking paper. Sprinkle parmesan in a thin layer on tray; flatten slightly. Bake for 8 minutes or until browned lightly. Cool on tray. Break into pieces when cold.

Test Kitchen
NOTES

You can use 1.6kg
(11 cups) frozen corn
kernels to save time.

soft polenta with mixed mushrooms

PREP + COOK TIME 20 MINUTES • SERVES 4

2 cups (500ml) milk

2 cups (500ml) vegetable stock

1 cup (170g) instant polenta

½ cup (40g) grated parmesan

100g (3 ounces) butter, chopped

200g (6½ ounces) swiss brown mushrooms, sliced thinly

200g (6½ ounces) button mushrooms, sliced thinly

3 shallots (75g), chopped finely

1 fresh long red chilli, sliced thinly

100g (3 ounces) oyster mushrooms, halved

2 cloves garlic, crushed

100g (3 ounces) baby spinach leaves

½ cup (70g) roasted hazelnuts, chopped coarsely

1 Bring milk and stock to the boil in a large saucepan. Gradually add polenta, stirring; cook, stirring occasionally, over medium heat, for 10 minutes or until polenta is thick and smooth. Stir in parmesan and 40g (1½ ounces) of the butter until melted. Season to taste; cover to keep warm.

2 Meanwhile, heat remaining butter in a large frying pan over high heat; cook swiss brown and button mushrooms, shallots and chilli, stirring occasionally, until browned lightly. Add oyster mushrooms and garlic; cook, stirring, until softened. Add spinach and hazelnuts; toss well. Season to taste.

3 Serve polenta topped with mushroom mixture.

mexican beans with cornbread and avocado salsa

PREP + COOK TIME 1 HOUR (+ COOLING) · SERVES 6

1 tablespoon olive oil

1 large red onion (300g), chopped finely

1 medium red capsicum (bell pepper) (200g), chopped coarsely

1 medium green capsicum (bell pepper) (200g), chopped coarsely

800g (1½ pounds) canned four bean mix, rinsed, drained

30g (1 ounce) sachet taco spice mix

800g (1½ pounds) canned diced tomatoes

400g (12½ ounces) canned corn kernels, drained

1 large avocado (320g)

½ cup coarsely chopped coriander (cilantro)

1 tablespoon lime juice

1 long green chilli, sliced thinly

CORNBREAD

1¾ cups (300g) polenta (cornmeal)

1 cup (120g) grated cheddar

½ cup (75g) self-raising flour

2 tablespoons finely chopped fresh chives

1¾ cups (430ml) buttermilk

2 eggs, beaten lightly

125g (4 ounces) butter, melted, cooled

1 Make cornbread.

2 Meanwhile, heat oil in a deep large frying pan over medium heat; cook onion and capsicums, stirring, for 5 minutes or until onion is soft. Add beans and spice mix; cook, stirring, for 1 minute or until fragrant.

3 Add tomatoes and corn to pan; bring to the boil. Reduce heat; simmer, uncovered, for 7 minutes or until sauce thickens.

4 Coarsely chop avocado. Combine avocado, coriander, juice and half the chilli in a small bowl. Season to taste.

5 Divide bean mixture between serving plates; top with avocado salsa and remaining chilli. Serve with cornbread.

CORNBREAD Preheat oven to 180°C/350°F. Oil a 14cm x 23cm (5½-inch x 9¼-inch) loaf pan; line base and sides with baking paper, extending the paper 5cm (2 inches) over long sides. Combine polenta, cheddar, flour and chives in a large bowl. Stir in buttermilk, egg and butter to combine (do not over-mix). Spoon mixture into pan; level surface. Bake about 40 minutes. Stand in pan 5 minutes before turning, top-side up, onto a wire rack to cool.

Test Kitchen NOTES

Slice leftover cornbread and cook on a heated oiled grill plate (or grill or barbecue) until golden on both sides and heated through. Serve with soup, salad or poached eggs.

Test Kitchen
NOTES

Polenta can be prepared a day ahead; store, covered, in the fridge. Swap the fresh corn for a 420g can of drained corn kernels.

char-grilled polenta strips with corn salsa

PREP + COOK TIME 30 MINUTES (+ REFRIGERATION) • SERVES 4

cooking-oil spray

1 litre (4 cups) water

1 cup (170g) polenta

2 tablespoons wholegrain (seeded) mustard

CORN SALSA

2 trimmed corn cobs (500g)

1 medium red capsicum (bell pepper) (200g), chopped finely

1 medium red onion (170g), chopped finely

1 lebanese cucumber (130g), seeded, chopped finely

¼ cup coarsely chopped fresh flat-leaf parsley

1 teaspoon finely grated lime rind

⅓ cup (80ml) lime juice

2 teaspoons olive oil

2 cloves garlic, crushed

1 tablespoon sweet chilli sauce

1 Lightly spray a 23cm (9½-inch) square cake pan with cooking oil.

2 Bring the water to the boil in a small saucepan. Stir in polenta; cook, stirring, for 10 minutes or until polenta thickens, season. Stir in mustard; spread polenta into pan. Cover polenta; refrigerate 30 minutes or until firm.

3 Meanwhile, make corn salsa.

4 Turn polenta onto a board; cut into 12 rectangles. Lightly spray a heated grill plate (or grill or barbecue) with oil. Cook polenta until browned both sides; serve with salsa.

CORN SALSA Boil, steam or microwave corn until just tender. Drain; cool. Using a sharp knife, remove kernels from cob. Combine corn in a medium bowl with remaining ingredients.

polenta chips with prosciutto and roast tomatoes

PREP + COOK TIME 45 MINUTES (+ REFRIGERATION) • SERVES 4

3 cups (750ml) chicken stock

¾ cup (125g) instant polenta

1 cup (80g) finely grated parmesan

500g (1 pound) cherry truss tomatoes

2 tablespoons olive oil

4 slices prosciutto (60g)

1 sprig fresh rosemary

1 cup (180g) ligurian olives

Serve with wood-fired or Italian-style bread.

1 Grease a deep 20cm (8-inch) square cake pan; line base and sides with baking paper.

2 Bring stock to the boil in a medium saucepan; gradually stir in polenta. Reduce heat; cook, stirring, for 10 minutes or until polenta thickens. Remove from heat; stir in half the parmesan. Season to taste. Spread polenta in pan. Refrigerate 3 hours or overnight.

3 Preheat oven to 220°C/425°F. Line two oven trays with baking paper.

4 Remove polenta from pan; cut into 20 thick chips. Place chips on a tray; sprinkle with remaining parmesan, turn to coat. Bake for 30 minutes or until golden and crisp.

5 Meanwhile, place tomatoes on other tray, drizzle with half the oil; season. Roast in oven for last 7 minutes of polenta chip cooking time.

6 Heat remaining oil in a large frying pan over medium heat; cook prosciutto and rosemary, turning, until prosciutto is golden and crisp. Drain on paper towel.

7 Arrange polenta chips, prosciutto and tomatoes on a platter; top with rosemary and serve with olives.

Test Kitchen
NOTES

Use wet hands when rolling the dumplings to stop them sticking. Use a wide saucepan so there is more surface area for the dumplings to cook.

chilli beef with cornbread dumplings

PREP + COOK TIME 1 HOUR 10 MINUTES • SERVES 4

1 tablespoon olive oil

1 medium brown onion (150g), chopped coarsely

800g (1½ pounds) minced (ground) beef

3 cloves garlic, crushed

2 teaspoons each ground cumin and smoked paprika

½ teaspoon cayenne pepper

400g (12½ ounces) canned kidney beans, rinsed, drained

800g (1½ pounds) canned diced tomatoes

1 cup (250ml) beef stock

1 cup (250ml) water

1 tablespoon brown sugar

CORNBREAD DUMPLINGS

1⅓ cups (200g) self-raising flour

⅓ cup (55g) polenta

¼ cup (30g) coarsely grated cheddar

¼ cup (60g) creamed corn

1 egg, beaten lightly

½ cup (125ml) milk

1 Heat oil in a large saucepan; cook onion, beef, garlic and spices, stirring, until beef is browned.
2 Add beans to pan with tomatoes, stock, the water and sugar; bring to the boil. Reduce heat; simmer, uncovered, for 30 minutes, stirring occasionally. Season to taste.
3 Meanwhile, make cornbread dumplings.
4 Roll level tablespoons of the dumpling mixture into balls and place on top of beef mixture; cook, covered, for 15 minutes or until dumplings are cooked.

CORNBREAD DUMPLINGS Combine sifted flour, polenta and cheddar in a medium bowl; stir in corn, egg and milk.

chicken and tarragon pie with polenta crust

PREP + COOK TIME 1 HOUR 40 MINUTES
(+ REFRIGERATION) • SERVES 6

2 tablespoons olive oil

1kg (2 pounds) chicken thigh fillets, cut into 3cm (1¼-inch) pieces

1 large leek (500g), white part only, chopped coarsely

1 kumara (orange sweet potato) (400g), chopped coarsely

½ cup (125ml) dry white wine

½ cup (125ml) chicken stock

200g (6½ ounces) crème fraîche

1 tablespoon plain (all-purpose) flour

2 teaspoons finely chopped fresh tarragon

2 teaspoons polenta

POLENTA PASTRY

2 cups (300g) plain (all-purpose) flour

½ cup (80g) polenta

200g (6½ ounces) unsalted cold butter, chopped

2 eggs, beaten lightly

¼ cup (60ml) iced water

1 Make polenta pastry.

2 Meanwhile, heat half the oil in a large frying pan over medium heat; cook chicken, in batches, until browned. Drain on paper towel. Heat remaining oil in same pan; cook leek and kumara, stirring, about 3 minutes. Add wine and stock; cook, stirring occasionally, for 10 minutes or until most of the liquid has evaporated. Remove from heat; stir in chicken, combined crème fraîche and flour, then tarragon. Cool.

3 Cut pastry in half. Roll out one half on a floured work surface until large enough to line a deep 23cm (9¼-inch) springform pan or deep pie tin. Ease pastry into pan; press into base and side. Cover; refrigerate 1 hour.

4 Preheat oven to 200°C/400°F; heat an oven tray.

5 Spoon chicken mixture into pastry case; brush pastry edge with a little of the reserved egg mixture. Roll out remaining pastry on a floured work surface until large enough to cover filling. Lift pastry onto filling; press pastry together to join. Trim edge, then press to seal with a fork. Brush top of pie with remaining reserved egg mixture; sprinkle with polenta.

6 Place pie on hot tray; bake about 20 minutes. Reduce oven to 180°C/350°F; bake a further 25 minutes or until pastry is golden. Stand pie in pan 10 minutes before serving.

POLENTA PASTRY Process sifted flour, polenta and butter until mixture resembles breadcrumbs. Combine egg and the iced water; reserve 1 tablespoon for brushing. Add remaining egg mixture to flour mixture, process until pastry begins to come together. Turn onto a work surface; knead lightly into a ball. Wrap in plastic wrap; refrigerate 2 hours.

Serve with mixed green peas and beans.

4 ways with POLENTA

soft polenta

PREP + COOK TIME 20 MINUTES • **SERVES** 6

Bring 3 cups milk and 2 cups chicken stock to the boil in a large saucepan. Gradually add 2 cups polenta, stirring constantly. Reduce heat; simmer, stirring, for 10 minutes or until polenta thickens. Stir in an extra 1 cup milk and ¼ cup finely grated parmesan until cheese melts. Serve topped with extra finely grated parmesan, if you like.

cheesy pesto polenta

PREP + COOK TIME 20 MINUTES • **SERVES** 6

Bring 3 cups milk and 2 cups chicken stock to the boil in a large saucepan. Gradually add 2 cups polenta, stirring constantly. Reduce heat; simmer, stirring, for 10 minutes or until polenta thickens. Stir in an extra 1 cup milk, 150g (4½ ounces) chunky basil dip and ¼ cup finely grated parmesan until cheese melts. Serve topped with extra finely grated parmesan, if you like.

lemon thyme polenta

PREP + COOK TIME 20 MINUTES • **SERVES** 6

Bring 3 cups milk and 2 cups chicken stock to
the boil in a large saucepan. Gradually add 2 cups
polenta, stirring constantly. Reduce heat, stir
in 2 teaspoons lemon thyme leaves; simmer, for
10 minutes or until polenta thickens. Stir in an
extra 1 cup milk, 1 teaspoon finely grated lemon
rind and ¼ cup finely grated parmesan until
cheese melts. Serve topped with strips of lemon
rind, if you like.

olive polenta

PREP + COOK TIME 20 MINUTES • **SERVES** 6

Bring 3 cups milk and 2 cups chicken stock to
the boil in a large saucepan. Gradually add 2 cups
polenta, stirring constantly. Reduce heat; simmer,
stirring, for 10 minutes or until polenta thickens.
Stir in an extra 1 cup milk, 75g (2½ ounces) coarsely
chopped pitted kalamata olives and ¼ cup finely
grated parmesan until cheese melts. Serve topped
with extra finely grated parmesan, if you like.

cracked wheat and couscous

spicy roast pumpkin with lamb

PREP + COOK TIME 1 HOUR 30 MINUTES • SERVES 6

¾ cup (150g) cracked wheat

2 tablespoons coarsely chopped fresh flat-leaf parsley

2 tablespoons coarsely chopped fresh thyme

2 tablespoons finely grated lemon rind

2 cloves garlic, crushed

2 tablespoons olive oil

1.4kg (2¾-pound) small jap pumpkin, unpeeled, cut into small wedges

1 cup (280g) Greek-style yoghurt

2 teaspoons sumac

6 thyme sprigs, torn, extra

LAMB TOPPING

1 tablespoon olive oil

1 medium onion (150g), chopped finely

1 teaspoon ground cinnamon

½ teaspoon cayenne pepper

300g (9½ ounces) minced (ground) lamb

1 tablespoon pomegranate molasses

1 Cook cracked wheat in a medium saucepan of boiling water about 10 minutes (it will be not quite cooked). Drain; rinse. Place wheat in a medium bowl; cool 15 minutes. Stir in chopped herbs, rind, garlic and oil; season to taste.

2 Preheat oven to 180°C/350°F. Line a large oven tray with baking paper.

3 Place pumpkin, skin-side down, on tray; spoon wheat mixture into the hollow of each wedge. Bake, uncovered, about 30 minutes; cover with foil, bake a further 30 minutes or until pumpkin is tender.

4 Meanwhile, make lamb topping.

5 Spoon lamb topping over pumpkin wedges; serve topped with yoghurt, sumac and extra thyme.

LAMB TOPPING Heat oil in a frying pan over medium heat; cook onion, cinnamon and cayenne, stirring about 3 minutes. Increase heat to high, add lamb; cook, stirring occasionally, for 5 minutes or until browned and cooked through. Stir in molasses; season to taste.

baked salmon fillets with tahini sauce and tabbouleh

PREP + COOK TIME 40 MINUTES · SERVES 4

4 x 150g (4½-ounce) salmon fillets, skinned

1½ teaspoons sumac

2 tablespoons extra virgin olive oil

TABBOULEH

½ cup (80g) coarse cracked wheat

1½ cups (375ml) water

2 green onions (scallions), sliced thinly

1 medium tomato (150g), chopped coarsely

1 cup firmly packed fresh flat-leaf parsley leaves, chopped coarsely

¼ cup firmly packed fresh mint leaves, chopped coarsely

1 tablespoon lemon juice

TAHINI SAUCE

½ cup (140g) Greek-style yoghurt

1½ tablespoons tahini

1 clove garlic, crushed

2 teaspoons lemon juice

1 Make tabbouleh, then tahini sauce.

2 Preheat oven to 200°C/400°F.

3 Line an oven tray with baking paper. Place salmon on tray, sprinkle with 1 teaspoon of the sumac; drizzle with oil. Season. Bake for 12 minutes or until almost cooked through.

4 Serve salmon with tahini sauce and tabbouleh. Sprinkle with remaining sumac.

TABBOULEH Bring cracked wheat and the water to the boil in a small saucepan. Reduce heat to low; cook for 20 minutes or until tender. Drain. Place cracked wheat in a large bowl with onion, tomato, herbs and juice; toss to combine. Season.

TAHINI SAUCE Whisk ingredients in a small bowl until combined; season to taste.

Make the tabbouleh and tahini sauce several hours ahead; store in the refrigerator until ready to use.

jewelled couscous salad

PREP + COOK TIME 15 MINUTES • SERVES 4

Test Kitchen NOTES

Fresh pomegranate seeds can sometimes be found in packs in the fridge section of supermarkets or good greengrocers. This recipe can be made several hours ahead; add dressing close to serving.

180g (5½ ounces) persian fetta in oil

1½ cups (300g) couscous

1½ cups (375ml) boiling water

½ cup (70g) shelled pistachios

½ cup loosely packed fresh coriander (cilantro) leaves, chopped coarsely

½ cup loosely packed fresh flat-leaf parsley leaves, chopped coarsely

3 green onions (scallions), sliced thinly

⅓ cup (50g) raisins

¼ cup (60ml) lemon juice

1 teaspoon sumac

⅓ cup (70g) pomegranate seeds

1 Drain oil from fetta into a jug or bowl; reserve ¼ cup of the oil.

2 Combine couscous with the boiling water and 1 tablespoon of the fetta oil in a large heatproof bowl, cover; stand 5 minutes or until liquid is absorbed, fluffing occasionally with a fork.

3 Meanwhile, place pistachios in a small frying pan; stir over medium heat until toasted lightly. Transfer pistachios to a chopping board, cool slightly; chop coarsely. Stir pistachios, herbs, onion and raisins into couscous; season to taste.

4 Whisk remaining fetta oil in a jug or small bowl with juice and sumac; season to taste.

5 Add dressing and pomegranate seeds to salad; toss gently to combine.

6 Transfer salad to a platter; top with crumbled fetta. Sprinkle with a little extra sumac, if you like.

moroccan lamb cutlets with couscous salad

2 teaspoons ras el hanout

⅓ cup (80ml) olive oil

12 french-trimmed lamb cutlets (600g)

1 medium green capsicum (bell pepper) (200g)

1 medium yellow capsicum (bell pepper) (200g)

1 medium red capsicum (bell pepper) (200g)

2 cups (500ml) water

30g (1 ounce) butter

1 teaspoon sea salt flakes

2 cups (400g) couscous

1½ tablespoons finely chopped preserved lemon rind

¼ cup torn fresh flat-leaf parsley leaves

200g (6½ ounces) hummus

1 Preheat grill (broiler).

2 Combine ras el hanout and half the oil in a large bowl; add lamb, turn to coat in mixture.

3 Quarter capsicums; discard seeds and membranes. Place, skin-side up, on a foil-lined oven tray, drizzle with remaining oil. Place under hot grill for 15 minutes or until skin blisters and blackens. Cover capsicum with plastic wrap or paper, leave 5 minutes; peel away skin, then slice thinly.

4 Meanwhile, bring the water, butter and salt to the boil in a medium saucepan. Stir in couscous; cover, stand 5 minutes. Fluff with a fork.

5 Combine couscous, capsicum, preserved lemon and parsley in a large bowl.

6 Cook lamb on a heated oiled chargrill plate (or grill or barbecue) for 4 minutes each side or until cooked as desired.

7 Spoon hummus into a small serving bowl; sprinkle with a little extra ras el hanout. Serve lamb with couscous salad and hummus.

Test Kitchen NOTES

Ras el hanout is a blend of 30 or more Moroccan spices which includes cardamom, mace, nutmeg, anise, cinnamon, ginger, pepper and turmeric. You can use a Moroccan seasoning instead or an equal mix of ground cumin and ground coriander.

couscous, red cabbage and walnut salad

PREP + COOK TIME 25 MINUTES • SERVES 4

3 cups (600g) couscous

3 cups (750ml) boiling water

⅓ cup (35g) walnuts, chopped coarsely

2 tablespoons olive oil

200g (6½ ounces) red cabbage, shredded thinly

⅓ cup (55g) sultanas

100g (3 ounces) fetta, crumbled

100g (3 ounces) baby rocket (arugula) leaves

DRESSING

¼ cup (60ml) olive oil

2 tablespoons lemon juice

1 tablespoon dijon mustard

1 Combine couscous with the boiling water in a large heatproof bowl; cover, stand 5 minutes. Fluff with a fork.

2 Meanwhile, make dressing.

3 Heat a large frying pan over high heat; cook walnuts, stirring, for 3 minutes or until roasted. Add oil, cabbage and sultanas; cook, stirring, a further 3 minutes or until cabbage begins to wilt.

4 Place cabbage mixture and couscous in a large heatproof bowl with fetta, rocket and dressing; toss gently to combine. Season to taste.

DRESSING Place ingredients in a screw-top jar; shake well. Season to taste.

moroccan carrots with chickpeas and spinach couscous

PREP + COOK TIME 30 MINUTES · SERVES 4

10 baby carrots (200g)

1 tablespoon olive oil

2 teaspoons ground cumin

1 teaspoon ground paprika

1 teaspoon caster (superfine) sugar

½ cup (125ml) water

1¼ cups (250g) couscous

1¼ cups (310ml) boiling water

30g (1 ounce) butter, chopped

400g (12½ ounces) canned chickpeas (garbanzo beans), rinsed, drained

1 tablespoon lemon juice

50g (1½ ounces) baby spinach leaves, shredded

1 cup loosely packed fresh coriander (cilantro) leaves

1 Trim and peel carrots, leaving 3cm (1¼ inches) of the stem.
2 Heat oil in a medium saucepan over a medium heat; cook spices for 30 seconds or until fragrant. Add carrots, sugar and the water; season to taste. Bring to the boil; simmer, partially covered, for 12 minutes or until carrots are tender.
3 Meanwhile, combine couscous with the boiling water in a large heatproof bowl; cover; stand 3 minutes. Fluff with a fork. Cover, stand a further 3 minutes; fluff with a fork. Stir in butter; season to taste.
4 Add chickpeas to pan with carrots; cook, covered, for 3 minutes or until heated through. Stir in juice.
5 Stir spinach through couscous; spoon onto a shallow serving dish. Top with carrot mixture and coriander.

Serve with Greek-style yoghurt and harissa.

couscous with spiced eggplant and lemony yoghurt

PREP + COOK TIME 35 MINUTES • SERVES 4

4 medium eggplants (1.2kg), halved, sliced thinly

4 cloves garlic, crushed

1 tablespoon za'atar

3 teaspoons ground cumin

2 teaspoons each ground coriander and turmeric

¾ teaspoon chilli flakes

½ cup (125ml) olive oil

⅓ cup (80ml) cold water

1½ cups (300g) couscous

1 tablespoon extra virgin olive oil

1½ cups (375ml) boiling water

½ cup loosely packed fresh coriander (cilantro) sprigs

LEMONY YOGHURT

1 cup (280g) plain yoghurt

1 tablespoon finely grated lemon rind

1 tablespoon lemon juice

1 clove garlic, crushed

1 Preheat oven to 200°C/400°F.

2 Place eggplant, garlic, spices and chilli in a large roasting pan; drizzle with combined olive oil and the cold water. Roast for 25 minutes, stirring halfway through, or until eggplant is golden and tender. Season to taste.

3 Meanwhile, place couscous in a heatproof bowl, drizzle with extra virgin olive oil; using your fingertips, rub oil into couscous. Stir in the boiling water; cover, stand 10 minutes. Fluff with a fork; season to taste.

4 Make lemony yoghurt.

5 Serve couscous topped with eggplant mixture, lemony yoghurt, coriander and a little extra za'atar.

LEMONY YOGHURT Combine ingredients in a small bowl.

pumpkin tabbouleh

PREP + COOK TIME 35 MINUTES • SERVES 2

200g (6½ ounces) coarsely chopped pumpkin

½ small red onion (50g), sliced thickly

1 teaspoon olive oil

1 cup (250ml) water

⅓ cup (55g) cracked wheat

½ cup fresh flat-leaf parsley

180g (5½ ounces) cherry tomatoes, halved

2 tablespoons lemon juice

1 clove garlic, crushed

1 Preheat oven to 220°C/425°F.

2 Line an oven tray with baking paper. Combine pumpkin and onion on tray; drizzle with oil. Bake for 20 minutes or until tender. Cool; transfer to a large bowl.

3 Meanwhile, bring the water to the boil in a small saucepan. Add cracked wheat; reduce heat, simmer, covered, for 15 minutes or until tender. Remove from heat; stand 10 minutes. Cool; transfer to the bowl with vegetables.

4 Combine parsley and tomato with pumpkin and cracked wheat mixture.

5 Combine juice and garlic, drizzle over tabbouleh; toss gently to combine.

zucchini and mint couscous salad

½ cup (100g) wholegrain couscous

½ cup (125ml) boiling water

2 small zucchini (180g), sliced thickly

½ cup fresh mint leaves

¼ cup crumbled fetta

1 tablespoon olive oil

2 teaspoons each finely grated lemon rind
and lemon juice

1 Combine couscous and the boiling water in a
medium bowl; cover, stand 5 minutes, fluff with
a fork occasionally.
2 Cook zucchini on a heated oiled grill plate (or
grill or barbecue) for 2 minutes each side or until
tender and browned.
3 Combine zucchini, couscous, mint, fetta, oil and
rind and lemon juice in a large bowl.

This is great as a
side dish with grilled
meat or fish.

lamb skewers with zucchini and moghrabieh salad

PREP + COOK TIME 50 MINUTES (+ REFRIGERATION) • SERVES 4

½ cup (125ml) pomegranate molasses

¼ cup (60ml) water

¼ cup (55g) brown sugar

2 tablespoons red wine vinegar

1 tablespoon olive oil

2 cloves garlic, crushed

1 teaspoon dried mint leaves

800g (1½ pounds) lamb rump steaks, trimmed, cut into 3cm (1¼-inch) pieces

ZUCCHINI AND MOGHRABIEH SALAD

1 cup (200g) moghrabieh

2 cups (500ml) water

2 medium zucchini (240g), sliced

2½ tablespoons olive oil

¼ cup (35g) flaked almonds, toasted

¼ cup firmly packed fresh mint leaves

1 small red onion (100g), sliced thinly

2 tablespoons red wine vinegar

1 Combine pomegranate molasses, the water, sugar, vinegar, oil, garlic and mint in a large bowl; season to taste.

2 Add lamb to bowl; toss to coat. Cover; refrigerate 1 hour or overnight.

3 Make zucchini and moghrabieh salad.

4 Thread lamb onto eight skewers; reserve marinade. Season lamb. Cook skewers on a heated oiled grill plate (or grill or barbecue) over medium heat for 6 minutes for medium, brushing with marinade every 2 minutes, or until browned all over and cooked as desired.

5 Meanwhile, place remaining marinade in a small saucepan; bring to the boil. Simmer, uncovered, for 5 minutes or until reduced slightly.

6 Spoon marinade over lamb; serve skewers with zucchini and moghrabieh salad.

ZUCCHINI AND MOGHRABIEH SALAD Bring moghrabieh and the water to the boil in a medium saucepan over high heat. Reduce heat to low; cook, covered, for 20 minutes or until tender. Drain. Meanwhile, combine zucchini with 1 tablespoon of the oil; cook on a heated grill plate or (grill or barbecue) over high heat for 2 minutes each side or until browned. Place moghrabieh and zucchini in a large bowl with almonds, mint, onion, vinegar and remaining oil; toss gently to combine. Season to taste.

Test Kitchen
NOTES

Pomegranate molasses is available from some major supermarkets, delicatessens and specialty food stores. When in season, add a handful of pomegranate seeds to the salad. If using wooden skewers, soak in cold water for 1 hour first.

Moghrabieh is a pearl-sized couscous available from delicatessens, specialty food stores and some supermarkets.

Test Kitchen
NOTES

This easy cracked wheat pilaf is a great side for any barbecued meat or fish. If reheating leftover pilaf, add a little boiling water as it tends to thicken when standing. You can marinate the chicken a day ahead; store, covered, in the fridge. You could add some ground coriander and a pinch of ground chilli to the marinade. This recipe can be doubled to serve 4.

turkish chicken kebabs with tomato wheat pilaf

PREP + COOK TIME 30 MINUTES (+ REFRIGERATION) • SERVES 2

1 cup (280g) plain yoghurt

1 clove garlic, crushed

1 teaspoon ground cumin

300g (9½ ounces) chicken thigh fillets, trimmed, cut into 3cm (1¼-inch) cubes

2 tablespoons fresh flat-leaf parsley leaves

TOMATO WHEAT PILAF

2 teaspoons olive oil

1 small brown onion (80g), chopped finely

¾ cup (120g) cracked wheat

1½ cups (325ml) water

1 tablespoon tomato paste

CUCUMBER SALAD

½ lebanese cucumber (65g), sliced thinly

1 medium tomato (150g), sliced thinly

¼ small red onion (25g), sliced thinly

1 Combine yoghurt and garlic in a shallow bowl; reserve half the mixture. Stir cumin into remaining yoghurt mixture; add chicken, rub all over to coat in mixture. Cover, refrigerate 30 minutes.

2 Meanwhile, make tomato wheat pilaf and cucumber salad.

3 Thread chicken onto four small skewers. Cook chicken on a heated oiled grill plate (or grill or barbecue) for 8 minutes, turning occasionally, or until cooked through.

4 Serve chicken skewers with tomato wheat pilaf, cucumber salad, reserved garlic yoghurt and parsley.

TOMATO WHEAT PILAF Heat oil in a medium saucepan over medium-high heat; cook onion, stirring, for 3 minutes or until softened. Stir in wheat, the water and paste. Bring to the boil, then reduce heat; simmer, covered, for 15 minutes or until liquid is absorbed. Remove from heat; stand, covered, 10 minutes.

CUCUMBER SALAD Combine ingredients in a small bowl.

4 ways with
COUSCOUS

lemon pistachio couscous

PREP + COOK TIME 15 MINUTES • **SERVES** 4

Combine 1 cup couscous, ¾ cup boiling water, 2 teaspoons finely grated lemon rind and ¼ cup lemon juice in a medium heatproof bowl. Cover; stand 5 minutes or until liquid is absorbed, fluffing with a fork occasionally. Meanwhile, dry-fry ½ cup pistachios in a heated small frying pan until fragrant; remove from pan, chop coarsely. Heat 2 teaspoons olive oil in same pan, add 1 clove crushed garlic and 1 finely chopped small red onion; cook, stirring, until onion softens. Fluff couscous then stir pistachios, onion mixture and ½ cup shredded fresh mint through couscous.

preserved lemon and olive couscous

PREP TIME 15 MINUTES • **SERVES** 6

Combine 1¼ cups couscous with 1¼ cups boiling water and 1 tablespoon oil in a large heatproof bowl, cover; stand 5 minutes or until water is absorbed, fluffing with a fork occasionally. Stir 400g (12½ ounces) rinsed, drained canned chickpeas (garbanzo beans), ½ cup coarsely chopped seeded green olives, 2 tablespoons lemon juice, 3 thinly sliced green onions (scallions), 2 tablespoons finely chopped fresh flat-leaf parsley and 1 tablespoon thinly sliced preserved lemon rind into couscous. Season to taste.

spicy red couscous

PREP + COOK TIME 15 MINUTES • SERVES 6

Heat 1 tablespoon olive oil in a medium saucepan,
add 2 teaspoons harissa paste, 2 teaspoons sweet
paprika and 2 thinly sliced green onions (scallions);
cook, stirring, for 2 minutes or until fragrant. Add
1 cup chicken stock and ½ cup water; bring to the
boil. Remove from heat, add 1½ cups couscous; cover,
stand 5 minutes or until liquid is absorbed, fluffing
with a fork occasionally. Stir 1 tablespoon lemon juice
into couscous; season to taste. Serve sprinkled with
2 finely sliced green onions.

test kitchen notes

Harissa is a hot paste;
there are many different brands
available on the market, and the
strengths vary enormously.

pine nut and dried fig couscous

PREP + COOK TIME 15 MINUTES • SERVES 4

Bring 1 cup chicken stock to the boil in a medium
saucepan. Remove from heat, add 1 cup couscous,
cover; stand 5 minutes or until liquid is absorbed,
fluffing with a fork occasionally. Stir ⅔ cup coarsely
chopped dried figs, ½ cup toasted pine nuts,
2 teaspoons finely grated lemon rind, ¼ cup lemon
juice and ¼ cup finely chopped fresh flat-leaf
parsley into couscous; season to taste.

test kitchen notes

Add your favourite dried fruit
or nuts to the couscous.
Serve warm or cold.

Cooking TECHNIQUES

preparing asparagus

To snap the woody end off the asparagus, hold it close to the base and bend it until it snaps. Discard the woody end and then trim the asparagus with a vegetable peeler.

crushing garlic

Press garlic firmly with the flat blade of a large knife (top) crushing the clove. Simply pull off the papery skin. A garlic press (bottom) removes and leaves the skin behind while crushing the garlic.

trimming beetroot

Cut the stems of beetroot to 2cm (¾ inch) from the bulb. Don't trim the beard at the base of the plant as this stops the colour from bleeding during cooking.

removing corn kernels

Remove the husk (the outer covering) and the silk (the soft silky inner threads) then trim one side of the corn cob so it lies flat. Use a large flat-bladed knife to cut down the cob, close to the core, to remove the kernels.

slicing vegies thinly

Cutting cucumber, zucchini, carrots, etc. into thin ribbons gives long thin, uniform slices. Use a vegetable peeler to do this. Applying more pressure on the peeler gives a thicker slice.

segmenting oranges

Cut top and bottom from orange with a small sharp knife. Cut remaining rind and white pith from orange, following the curve of the fruit. Holding the orange over a bowl, cut down both sides of the white membrane to release each segment.

seeding pomegranate

Cut a medium pomegranate in half then turn one half upside down over a bowl. Hit the shell with a wooden spoon – the seeds usually fall out easily. Repeat with the other half.

trimming green onion

Pull the papery skin towards the root and off the onion. Cut the root end off, then slice the white end of the onion as directed in the recipe. The green end can be used to garnish the dish.

making a thin omelette

Lightly whisk eggs then pour into a heated lightly-oiled wok (or large frying pan). Tilt the wok to cover the base with the egg; cook until the egg is set.

slicing chilli

The seeds are the heat source so, if you are intolerant of high heat levels, remove the seeds and membranes, or use less chilli. Don't touch your face after touching chilli as it can burn your eyes and mouth.

toasting nuts

Add nuts to a small dry frying pan; cook, stirring occasionally, over medium heat for 4 minutes or until golden. Remove from pan; cool.

slicing capsicum

Cut the top and bottom off and stand capsicum on one end; slice down removing all the flesh. Remove and discard the seeds and membranes, then slice the flesh.

GLOSSARY

BARLEY a nutritious grain used in soups and stews. Hulled barley, the least processed, is high in fibre. Pearl barley has had the husk removed then been steamed and polished so that only the 'pearl' of the original grain remains, much the same as white rice.

BEANS

broad (fava) also called windsor and horse beans; available dried, fresh, canned and frozen. Fresh should be peeled twice (discarding the outer long green pod and the beige-green tough inner shell); frozen beans have had their pods removed but the beige shell still needs removal.

cannellini a small white bean similar in appearance and flavour to other white beans (great northern, navy or haricot), all of which can be substituted for the other. Available dried or canned.

edamame fresh green baby soya beans; available, fresh and frozen, from major supermarkets and Asian grocery stores.

four bean mix a canned mixture of kidney beans, baby lima beans, chickpeas and butter beans.

kidney medium-sized red bean, slightly floury in texture, yet sweet in flavour.

sprouts also known as bean shoots; tender new growths of assorted beans and seeds germinated for consumption.

BEETROOT (beets) also known as red beets; a firm, round root vegetable.

baby young beets have a finer and more tender texture than beetroots. The green leafy portion of the beet is also edible and its texture is similar to that of spinach.

BROCCOLINI a cross between broccoli and chinese kale; long asparagus-like stems with a long loose floret, both completely edible. Resembles broccoli but is milder and sweeter in taste.

BUTTER use salted or unsalted (sweet) butter; 125g is equal to one stick of butter (4 ounces).

CAPERS grey-green buds of a warm climate shrub (usually Mediterranean); sold dried and salted or pickled in a vinegar brine. Whether packed in brine or in salt, capers must be rinsed well before using.

baby those picked early are very small, fuller-flavoured and more expensive than the full-size ones.

CAPSICUM (bell pepper) also known as just 'pepper'. Comes in many colours: red, green, yellow, orange and purplish-black. Be sure to discard seeds and membranes before use.

CHEESE

cheddar the most common cow's milk 'tasty' cheese; should be aged, hard and have a pronounced bite.

fetta Greek in origin; a crumbly textured goat- or sheep-milk cheese having a sharp, salty taste. Ripened and stored in salted whey.

fetta, persian a soft, creamy fetta marinated in a blend of olive oil, garlic, herbs and spices. It is available from most larger supermarkets.

goat's made from goats' milk; it has an earthy taste. Is available in both soft and firm textures, in various shapes and sizes, and sometimes rolled in ash or herbs.

gorgonzola a creamy blue cheese with a mild, sweet taste.

haloumi a firm, cream-coloured sheep-milk cheese matured in brine; haloumi can be grilled or fried, briefly, without breaking down. Should be eaten while still warm as it becomes tough and rubbery on cooling.

mascarpone a cultured cream product made in much the same way as yoghurt. Whitish to creamy yellow in colour, with a soft, creamy texture and a rich, sweet, slightly acidic, taste.

mozzarella soft, spun-curd cheese. It originated in southern Italy where it was traditionally made from water-buffalo milk. Now, generally made from cows' milk, it is the most popular pizza cheese.

parmesan also called parmigiano; this hard, grainy cows'-milk cheese originated in Italy. Reggiano is the best variety.

pecorino the generic Italian name for cheeses made from sheep milk; hard, white to pale-yellow cheeses. If you can't find it, use parmesan.

ricotta a soft, sweet, moist, white cows'-milk cheese with a low fat content and a slightly grainy texture. The name roughly translates as 'cooked again' and refers to ricotta's manufacture from whey, which is itself a by-product of other cheese making.

CHIA SEEDS an unprocessed, wholegrain seed with a mild, nutty flavour.

CHICKPEAS (garbanzo beans) also called hummus or channa; an irregularly round, sandy-coloured legume. They remain firm after cooking, with a floury mouth-feel and robust nutty flavour; available canned or dried (reconstitute for several hours in cold water before use).

CHILLI generally, the smaller the chilli, the hotter it is. Use rubber gloves when seeding and chopping fresh chillies as they can burn your skin. Removing seeds and membranes lessens the heat level.

long available both fresh and dried; a generic term used for any moderately hot, long (6-8cm/2¼-3¼ inch), thin chilli.

red thai small, hot and bright red. Substitute with fresh serrano chillies.

CHOY SUM also known as pakaukeo or flowering cabbage, a member of the buk choy family; easy to identify with its long stems, light green leaves and yellow flowers. Stems and leaves are both edible, steamed or stir-fried.

CINNAMON available in pieces (called sticks or quills) and ground into powder; one of the world's most common spices, used as a sweet, fragrant flavouring for both sweet and savoury foods.

COCONUT

flakes dried flaked coconut flesh.

milk not the liquid found inside the fruit (coconut water), but the diluted liquid from the second pressing of the white flesh of a mature coconut (the first pressing produces coconut cream).

CORIANDER (cilantro) also known as pak chee or chinese parsley; a bright-green leafy herb with a pungent flavour. Both the stems and roots of coriander are also used; wash well before using. Also available ground or as seeds; these should not be substituted for fresh coriander as the tastes are completely different.

CORN versatile and nutritious, corn is eaten both as a vegetable and as a grain but is actually classified as a fruit.

COUSCOUS a fine, grain-like cereal product made from semolina; it swells to three or four times its original size when liquid is added. Eaten like rice with a tagine or as a side dish.

moghrabieh a pearl-sized couscous available from delicatessens, specialty food stores and some supermarkets.

CRACKED WHEAT the whole wheat berry broken during milling into a cereal product of varying degrees of coarseness; used extensively in breadmaking and Middle-Eastern cooking.

CUMIN a spice also known as zeera or comino; has a spicy, nutty flavour.

CURRY LEAVES available fresh or dried and have a mild curry flavour.

CURRY PASTES commercially made pastes vary in strengths and flavours. Use whichever one you feel best suits your spice-level tolerance.

panang based on the curries of Penang, an island off the north-west coast of Malaysia, close to the Thai border. A complex, sweet and milder variation of red curry paste; good with seafood and for adding to soups and salad dressings.

DUKKAH an Egyptian specialty spice mixture made up of roasted nuts, seeds and an array of aromatic spices.

EGGPLANT also known as aubergine. Ranging in size from tiny to very large and in colour from pale green to deep purple. Can also be purchased char-grilled, packed in oil, in jars.

baby also known as finger or japanese eggplant; very small and slender so can be used without disgorging.

FENNEL also known as finocchio or anise; a white to very pale green-white, firm, crisp, roundish vegetable about 8-12cm in diameter. The bulb has a slightly sweet, anise flavour but the leaves have a much stronger taste. Also the name given to the dried seeds, which have a licorice flavour.

FISH SAUCE also called nam pla or nuoc nam; made from pulverised salted fermented fish, most often anchovies. Has a very pungent smell and strong taste, so use according to your taste level.

FLOUR

00 has a finer grain than plain flour, resulting in airy, light bread and soft, delicate pasta.

atta a fine wholemeal flour used in Indian flatbreads. It is available from most major supermarkets and Indian food stores.

bread also known as bakers' flour, has a higher protein content than plain flour, usually ranging from 12% to 16%. Recipes using bread flour require more kneading that plain flour.

chickpea (besan) made from ground chickpeas; also known as garam flour.

plain (all-purpose) a general unbleached wheat flour, the best for baking: the gluten content ensures a strong dough, for a light result.

rice very fine, almost powdery, gluten-free flour; made from ground white rice. Used in baking, as a thickener and in some Asian noodles and desserts. Another variety, made from glutinous sweet rice, is used for chinese dumplings and rice paper.

self-raising (self-rising) plain flour sifted with baking powder in the proportion of 1 cup flour to 2 teaspoons baking powder.

wholemeal also known as wholewheat flour; milled with the wheat germ intact so is higher in fibre and more nutritious than plain flour.

GAI LAN also known as chinese broccoli, gai larn, kanah, gai lum and chinese kale; appreciated more for its stems than its coarse leaves.

GARAM MASALA a blend of spices that includes cardamom, cinnamon, fennel, coriander, cloves and cumin. Black pepper and chilli can be added for heat.

GHEE a type of clarified butter where the milk solids are cooked until they are a golden brown, which imparts a nutty flavour and sweet aroma; this fat has a high smoking point so can be heated to a high temperature without burning. Used as a cooking medium in most Indian recipes. Available from many Indian supermarkets. Replace with clarified butter if you can't find it.

KAFFIR LIME LEAVES also known as bai magrood. Aromatic leaves of a citrus tree; two glossy dark green leaves joined end to end, forming a rounded hourglass shape. A strip of fresh lime peel may be substituted for each kaffir lime leaf.

KECAP MANIS a dark, thick sweet soy sauce used in most South-East Asian cuisines. The sweetness is derived from the addition of either molasses or palm sugar when brewed.

KUMARA (orange sweet potato) the Polynesian name of an orange-fleshed sweet potato often confused with yam.

LABNE a soft cheese made by salting plain (natural) yoghurt and draining it of whey for up to 2 days until it becomes thick enough to roll into small balls. These may be sprinkled with or rolled in chopped herbs or spices.

LEBANESE CUCUMBER short, slender and thin-skinned. Probably the most popular variety because of its tender, edible skin, tiny, yielding seeds and sweet, fresh flavoursome taste.

LEEK a member of the onion family, the leek resembles a green onion but is much larger and more subtle in flavour. Tender baby or pencil leeks can be eaten whole with minimal cooking, but adult leeks are usually trimmed of most of the green tops then chopped or sliced.

LENTILS (red, brown, yellow) dried pulses often identified by and named after their colour; also known as dhal.

french-style green a local cousin to the famous (and expensive) French lentils du puy; green-blue, tiny lentils with a nutty, earthy flavour and a hardy nature that allows them to be rapidly cooked without disintegrating.

LINSEED, SUNFLOWER AND ALMOND BLEND (LSA) a mixture of ground linseeds, sunflower seed kernels and almonds; available in health food shops or health food sections of supermarkets.

MUSHROOMS

button small, cultivated white mushrooms with a mild flavour.

dried porcini also known as cèpes; the richest-flavoured mushrooms. Expensive, but, because they're so strongly flavoured, only a small amount is required.

flat large, flat mushrooms with a rich earthy flavour. They are sometimes misnamed field mushrooms, which are wild mushrooms.

oyster also known as abalone; these grey-white mushrooms are shaped like a fan. They are prized for their smooth texture and subtle, oyster-like flavour.

shiitake although cultivated, they are large and meaty and have the earthiness and taste of wild mushrooms.

swiss brown also known as cremini or roman mushrooms; light brown mushrooms having a full-bodied flavour.

MUSTARD SEEDS available in black, brown or yellow varieties.

ONIONS

brown and white interchangeable; white onions have a more pungent flesh.

green (scallions) also known, incorrectly, as shallot; an immature onion picked before the bulb has formed. Has a long, bright-green edible stalk.

red also known as spanish, red spanish or bermuda onion; a sweet-flavoured, large, purple-red onion.

shallots also called french shallots, golden shallots or eschalots; small, brown-skinned, elongated members of the onion family.

PASTA

fettuccine fresh or dried ribbon pasta made from durum wheat, semolina and egg. Available plain or flavoured.

penne translated literally as 'quills'; ridged macaroni cut into short lengths on the diagonal.

risoni small rice-shape pasta; very similar to another small pasta, orzo.

spaghetti long, thin solid strands of pasta.

POLENTA also known as cornmeal; a flour-like cereal made of ground corn (maize). Also the name of the dish that is made from it.

POMEGRANATE dark-red, leathery-skinned fresh fruit about the size of an orange filled with hundreds of seeds, each wrapped in an edible lucent-crimson pulp having a unique tangy sweet-sour flavour.

POMEGRANATE MOLASSES not to be confused with pomegranate syrup or grenadine (which is used in cocktails); pomegranate molasses is thicker, browner and more concentrated in flavour – tart, sharp, slightly sweet and fruity. Buy from Middle-Eastern food stores or specialty food shops.

PRESERVED LEMON RIND a North African specialty; lemons are quartered and preserved in salt and lemon juice or water. To use, remove and discard the pulp, squeeze the juice from the rind, rinse the rind well, then slice thinly.

QUINOA pronounced 'keen-wa'; a gluten-free grain. It has a delicate, slightly nutty taste and chewy texture. Its cooking qualities are similar to rice. It spoils easily, so keep sealed in the fridge.

RADICCHIO a red-leafed Italian chicory, with a bitter taste, eaten raw and grilled. Comes in varieties that are named after their places of origin, such as round-headed Verona or long-headed Treviso.

RAS EL HANOUT a classic spice blend used in Moroccan cooking. The name means 'top of the shop' and is the very best spice blend a spice merchant has to offer. Most versions contain over a dozen spices, including cardamom, nutmeg, mace, cinnamon and ground chilli.

RICE

arborio small, round grain rice well-suited to absorb a large amount of liquid; the high level of starch makes it especially suitable for risottos.

basmati a white, fragrant long grain rice; the grains fluff up when cooked. Wash several times before cooking.

brown retains the high-fibre, nutritious bran coating that's removed from white rice when hulled. It takes longer to cook than white rice and has a chewier texture. Once cooked, the long grains stay separate, while the short grains are soft and stickier.

carnaroli a medium grain Italian rice traditionally used for making risotto. It differs from the more common arborio rice due to its higher starch content and firmer texture, as well as having a longer grain.

medium grain previously sold as calrose rice; extremely versatile rice that can be substituted for short or long grain rices if necessary.

rolled flattened rice grain rolled into flakes; looks similar to rolled oats.

sticky also known as sweet rice or glutinous rice; a short, fat grain having a chalky white centre. When cooked becomes soft and sticky, hence the name; requires long soaking and steaming.

SEMOLINA coarsely ground flour milled from durum wheat; the flour used in making gnocchi, pasta and couscous.

SNOW PEAS also called mange tout ('eat all'); a variety of garden pea, eaten pod and all

SPELT one of the world's most ancient grains; it has a nutty flavour similar to barley. It is sold as flour or whole berries and used in bread, pasta and baking.

SOY SAUCE also known as sieu; made from fermented soya beans. Several variations are available in supermarkets and Asian food stores. We use a mild Japanese variety in our recipes.

light fairly thin in consistency and, while pale, the saltiest tasting; used in dishes in which the natural colour of the ingredients is to be maintained. Not to be confused with salt-reduced or low-sodium soy sauces.

SPINACH also known as english spinach and, incorrectly, silver beet.

SUMAC a purple-red, astringent spice ground from berries growing on shrubs in the Mediterranean; adds a tart, lemony flavour to food. Available from spice shops and major supermarkets.

TAHINI a rich sesame-seed paste.

THICKENED CREAM (heavy) a whipping cream that contains a thickener. It has a minimum fat content of 35%.

VINEGAR

red wine based on a blend of fermented red wines.

rice wine made from fermented rice with no additives.

white wine made from a blend of white wines.

WATERCRESS a member of the cress family, a large group of peppery greens. Highly perishable, so must be used as soon as possible after purchase.

WOMBOK (napa cabbage) also known as peking cabbage, chinese cabbage or petsai; elongated in shape with pale green, crinkly leaves.

YOGHURT, GREEK-STYLE often made from sheep milk that is strained in a cloth (traditionally muslin) to remove the whey and to give it a thick, smooth, creamy consistency, almost like whipped cream.

ZA'ATAR a Middle Eastern herb and spice mixture which varies in makeup; however, it always includes thyme, ground sumac and, usually, toasted sesame seeds.

ZUCCHINI also called courgette; a small, pale- or dark-green or yellow vegetable.

INDEX

This book is published in 2015 by Octopus Publishing Group Limited
based on materials licensed to it by Bauer Media Books, Australia

Bauer Media Books is a division of Bauer Media Pty Limited.

54 Park St, Sydney; GPO Box 4088, Sydney, NSW 2001, Australia

phone (+61) 2 9282 8618; fax (+61) 2 9126 3702

www.awwcookbooks.com.au

MEDIA GROUP

BAUER MEDIA BOOKS

Publisher – Jo Runciman

Editorial & food director – Pamela Clark

Director of sales, marketing & rights – Brian Cearnes

Creative director – Hieu Chi Nguyen

Designer – Jeannel Cunanan

Junior editor – Amy Bayliss

Food editor – Emma Braz

Published and Distributed in the United Kingdom by Octopus Publishing Group

Endeavour House

189 Shaftesbury Avenue

London WC2H 8JY

phone (+44) (0) 207 632 5400; fax (+44) (0) 207 632 5405

info@octopus-publishing.co.uk;

www.octopusbooks.co.uk

Printed by Toppan Printing Co., Hong Kong

International foreign language rights, Brian Cearnes, Bauer Media Books bcearnes@bauer-media.com.au

A catalogue record for this book is available from the British Library.
ISBN: 978 1909770 270 (paperback)

THE AUSTRALIAN
Women's Weekly

ALSO FROM THE BEST-SELLING COOKERY SERIES OF ALL TIME

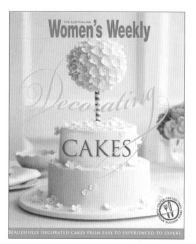

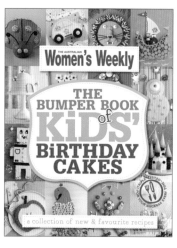

To order books visit www.octopusbooks.co.uk or telephone +44 (0)1903 828 503